C000265045

Australia

Berlitz Publishing Company, Inc.

Princeton   Mexico City   London   Eschborn   Singapore

Berlitz Trademark Reg. U.S. Patent Office and other countries
Marca Registrada

Text:	original text: Ken Bernstein
	revised by Peter Needham
Editor:	Media Content Marketing, Inc.
Photography:	Jon Davison; N.T. Tourist Commission pages 80, 111
Cover Photo:	Jon Davison
Layout:	Media Content Marketing, Inc.
Cartography:	Ortelius Design

Although the publisher tries to insure the accuracy of all the information in this book, changes are inevitable and errors may result. The publisher cannot be responsible for any resulting loss, inconvenience, or injury. If you find an error in this guide, please let the editors know by writing to Berlitz Publishing Company, 400 Alexander Park, Princeton, NJ 08540-6306.

ISBN 2-8315-7835-3

Printed in Italy
010/110 REV

CONTENTS

- A (☛) in the text denotes a highly recommended sight

Australia

AUSTRALIA AND THE AUSTRALIANS

Australia has bounded into the 21st century with optimistic exuberance, spurred on by the sensational Sydney 2000 Olympic Games.

"I invite you to suggest a more successful event anywhere in the peacetime history of mankind," effused US travel writer Bill Bryson, a keen Olympic spectator, in the London *Times.*

The Games focused unprecedented media attention on the "Land Down Under," a country which in many people's minds had always consisted of vague images: the Great Barrier Reef; the unforgiving Outback; and all those cute and bizarre Australian animals. It's true that the kangaroo, the koala, the wombat, the duck-billed platypus, and the Tasmanian devil exist nowhere else in the world outside zoos — and neither does anything resembling them. No wonder people remember them.

Media coverage of the Olympics helped broaden Australia's image and move it away from the "reef, desert, koalas, and crocs" stereotype. The Games became the most watched event in history, with more than 3.8 billion people worldwide tuning in. Between the sporting contests, viewers caught glimpses of Australia's people, beaches, cityscapes, and architecture. They liked what they saw.

Although the Games belonged to Sydney, Australia's biggest city, the benefits flowed widely. A record 4.9 million international tourists visited Australia in 2000 — 11 percent more than in 1999. The tourist boom shows no sign of slowing in the coming years; visitor arrivals are forecast to increase annually to 10 million by 2010, a figure equal to about half of Australia's population. In January 2001, the premiere episode of *Survivor II, The Australian Outback* was watched by 42 million US television viewers. That, and the pro-

gram's subsequent episodes, spurred even more interest in the great southern island continent.

It all represents a massive turnaround for a country which, for most of its history, has been little known and even less understood. A character in an Oscar Wilde play set in Queen Victoria's heyday summed up the foreigner's blurred impression of Australia: "It must be so pretty with all the dear little kangaroos flying about. Agatha has found it on the map."

Similarly fuzzy impressions persisted for decades. Australia is still perceived as a quirky, topsy-turvy land shared by eccentric marsupials and a laid-back human population that is fond of sun-bathing, surfing, and swilling cold beer.

Like most clichés, there's something to it. Aussies (pronounced *ozzies*), relish the outdoor life. Many radiate health and either possess or admire tanned muscles. If they're not actually at the beach, male Aussies are likely to be hiking, jogging, playing football (or at

Melbourne, Victoria's capital, glitters at twilight.

least listening to football or cricket on the radio), or they are out in the garden barbecuing beef or seafood. To complete the picture, there's usually an icy beer at hand to pacify the fiercest thirst. Australians may not be quite the world's most insatiable beer drinkers, but they're high in the league.

Prospectors seeking gold, opals, or other minerals still roam the stark Outback. In Australia's wild northern "Top End," enormous crocodiles and deadly snakes stalk unwary — and sometimes human — prey. Remote cattle farms are so big, cowboys conduct their roundups using a helicopter; one of the ranches is the size of Belgium.

But these startling facts represent only part of the truth. Camping vacations are as close as the overwhelming majority of Australians get to living in the bush. Australia is one of the world's most urbanized countries, with over 90 percent of its population living near the coast in the 10 biggest cities. More than one Australian in five lives in Sydney (population 4 million). Melbourne is approaching the same size. Other state capitals — Brisbane, Adelaide, and Perth — account for most of the rest of the population.

For many people, Australia's natural wonders, its odd wildlife and its far-flung open spaces still eclipse everything else. The vast and eerily beautiful Outback holds an almost hypnotic appeal. When best-selling thriller author Stephen King took a well-deserved short break from writing in 1997 and roared into Australia's wide-open expanses on a motorcycle, he described his sense of awe: "If you stop, the silence is incredible. You feel very small; you can almost hear God breathing."

Extraordinary wildlife wanders the Outback. Australia has a virtual monopoly on monotremes, the generic name for a type of mammal which includes the waddling, spine-covered echidna and the platypus, an egg-laying furry mammal with a duck-like beak. More familiar are Australia's marsupials, equipped with pouches to solve the baby-sitting problem. Bounding across the Australian landscape are numerous varieties of kangaroo, from small wallabies to giant red roos big enough to cow any heavyweight boxer. Another marsupial, the languid, furry koala, eschews violent exercise, spending its days drowsing in a eucalyptus-induced haze.

Birdwatchers here can count hundreds of species. Thrillingly colorful birds are as common as sparrows, and lyrical or humorous bird-calls provide every evening's country music. These indigenous stars have names like flowerpecker, honeyeater, and kookaburra, but the favorite bird of crossword puzzlers — the emu — can't sing or fly.

Australia has been isolated from other continents since it split from the remnants of the southern super-continent, Gondwana, about 40 million years ago. Cut off from the evolutionary mainstream, plants and animals developed in ways that have engrossed generations of scientists and astounded thousands of ordinary tourists.

For countless millennia, the only humans sharing the continent with these native animals were nomadic Aboriginal tribes. These first Australians are believed to have arrived from Asia, probably by boat, somewhere between 50,000 and 100,000 years ago — possibly even farther back. Australia's Aborigines lived within tribal boundaries they believed had been created by hero ancestors in a period called the Dreamtime. Aborigines built no permanent structures but lived in a manner that ensured their survival in a harsh environment.

Their lives changed little until European explorers began arriving in the 17th and 18th centuries. The colonial history of Australia began in 1770 when renowned English navigator Captain James Cook landed on Australia's east coast and claimed all the territory he charted for King George III. Shortly after Cook's arrival, the British decided Australia was an ideal place to send convicts and in 1787, Britain dispatched a soldier-and-convict fleet to colonize Australia, one of the furthest-flung points of its Empire.

The "Top End" of Western Australia is inhabited by huge crocodiles and poisonous snakes.

In a relatively short time, the British Empire had casually seized the traditional lands of Australia's dark-skinned hunter-gatherers. Aborigines were dispersed and decimated. Australia's indigenous people (who now represent about 1 percent of the country's population) did not gain the vote until 1962 and were not included in Australia's official census until 1967.

The fact that modern Australia can be traced back to chain gangs of convicted felons rather than to resolute idealists has left its mark on the national psyche, although the impact is fading. Australians were once notably defensive about their country, asking foreigners what they thought of it, then waiting anxiously for the answer. These days, Aussies are more relaxed about such matters. The descendants of convicts have long since been outnumbered by the descendants of free settlers, but if Australians can prove convict ancestry they do so eagerly—it's considered a mark of prestige.

The country has much to be proud of. In little more than 200 years, a tiny European settlement founded in conditions of brutality, servitude, and privation has prospered and transformed itself into a dynamic modern nation whose economy places it in the top 10 OECD countries in terms of gross domestic product. Tourism is the largest earner of foreign exchange and a major employer, accounting for 500,000 jobs directly, or almost seven percent of Australia's workforce.

Australia's geographical superlatives are clear-cut: It is the world's biggest island. More accurately, it is the smallest and least populous (about 19 million inhabitants) of the continents, and the only one housing a single nation. Australia occupies about the same area as the 48 mainland states of the United States, or about 24 times the area of the British Isles. Size is an important factor to consider if you're planning a "see-Australia-in-a-hurry" itinerary.

While Outback Australia includes regions of breathtaking natural beauty, much of the interior is arid, consisting of immense deserts and salt pans. Only nine percent of Australia is arable, which is why the settlement pattern has been so different from that of the United States, and why the population is so much smaller. Non-arable land is not necessarily unproductive; under the surface lie bauxite, coal, iron ore, copper, tin, silver, uranium, nickel, tungsten, lead, zinc, diamonds, natural gas, and oil.

Australia is the world's flattest continent, although the nation's summit, Mount Kosciuszko (elevation 2,228 m/7,308 ft), is almost as high as Mexico City. You can ski in the Australian Alps in August. The country's first ski club, the Kiandra Snow-Shoe Club, was founded in 1870—two years before the first clubs in the United States.

Australia is the driest continent, with only one river (the Murray) worthy of world ranking. The country's coastline of 36,735 km (almost 23,000 miles) includes many sweeping empty beaches where you can see nobody for a whole day or longer. You can dip a toe, or a surfboard, in legendary seas and oceans, among them the Coral Sea, the Timor Sea, the Indian Ocean, and the Southern Ocean.

Australia is a long way from northern-hemisphere population centers: 9,720 km (6,000 miles) from the United States, 17,820 (11,000) from Britain. But non-stop or one-stop flights make the going relatively easy. More distant in cultural terms are Australia's nearest neighbors, Indonesia and Papua New Guinea, a kangaroo's hop to the north. The Asian connection is becoming more important, not only politically and economically, but in human terms; a look at the faces on any city street shows the vastly increased flow of immigrants.

Over the past decade, cultural intermingling has revolutionized the national diet. Urban Australia enjoys a collage of culinary influences on fresh, high-quality ingredients. All state capitals have a lively café scene and at least one wine-growing area nearby, giving the chance to sample wines at the cellar door. Climatic diversity allows Australia to produce warm and cool-climate wines and to grow exotica such as rambutans, custard apples, mangoes, bok choy, mizuna and lychees, as well as more familiar apples, strawberries, blackberries, coconuts, and mandarins. In big cities like Sydney, Melbourne, or Brisbane,

The beaches of Brisbane beckon to sunworshippers.

you'll have no trouble finding restaurants serving excellently prepared cuisine from Thailand, Mexico, Cambodia, Japan, France, Lebanon, Turkey, or Italy. In smaller towns, the choice is more limited—you may have to settle for a meat pie, fish and chips, or chop suey!

Australia is home to some of the world's best-preserved wilderness areas. The World Heritage List currently includes 13 Australian regions, ranging from the Great Barrier Reef and the Tasmanian Wilderness to the Wet Tropics of Queensland and the Blue Mountains, the latter a day-trip from Sydney.

Australia's rainforests, healthy and diverse, form one of the world's best-preserved wilderness resources. From the lush, dense jungles of Tropical North Queensland, the rainforest region extends south to the planet's last great stand of temperate rainforest—the cool, moist forests of Tasmania.

A beast shows his aggressive side on a lush
Queensland crocodile farm.

Apart from their sheer beauty, Australia's rainforests contain about half of all Australian plant species, including "primitive" plant families providing direct links with the birth of flowering plants over 100 million years ago. At almost all Australian latitudes you'll see hardy trees of two main families. There are more than 500 types of eucalyptus, mostly gray-green, native to Australia, and 600 species of flowering acacia.

Some of Australia's most colorful sights exist under the sea. Divers go down under Down Under to admire the sort of fish you see in a collector's tropical tank—but in these seas they're 10 times bigger. Gorgeous angel fish and moorish idols glide past the enthralled skin diver's mask. Big-mouthed sharks and venomous scorpion fish may also turn up.

For enthusiasts of underwater spectacles, the most exciting place in the world is the Great Barrier Reef. This 1,944-km-long (1,200-mile-long) miracle—a living structure of coral—thrills the imagination in its immensity and in the intricate detail of brightly hued organisms shaped like antlers, flowers, fans, or brains. It's the world's biggest living thing. The most sublime tropical fish congregate here, too.

The reef, one of Australia's top-priority tourist destinations, has become ever more accessible. So has Ayers Rock, complete with its own airport and hotel complex. Australia's highly developed transport system puts the whole continent within reach: beaches and ski resorts, dynamic cities and Outback ghost towns.

Even among such a wealth of natural wonders, it's the people you meet who often leave the deepest impression. Australians generally are a friendly, no-nonsense bunch—direct and to the point. "Gidday mate!" is a cheery greeting used often, sometimes followed by "how ya goin', alright?" Americans detect Cockney or Irish overtones in the Australian accent—yet some visitors from Britain or Ireland swear they can identify an American influence.

Many Australian terms are unique, as likely to baffle a Briton or European as an American. "Don't come the raw prawn" is a picturesque example, fading now from general usage. It means "don't try to pull the wool over my eyes." The happy-go-lucky expression "she'll be right" has been largely supplanted by "no worries, mate", but they both mean the same thing—"it will all turn out OK!"

The Aussie sense of humor can bewilder newcomers. It's peppered with ironic understatements and playful contradictions, such as: "she's getting a bit warm" (as the shade temperature reaches 40°C or 104°F); "you're not wrong, mate" (an expression of enthusiastic agreement); or, "now there's a man who hates a drink" (meaning that the man is a heavy drinker).

Until recently, Australia was a man's world, where the missus stayed at home scrubbing the floor while the husband played football with his mates, talked macho, and drank a lot. Early in the 20th century, the popular Australian poet, Henry Lawson, explained this drinking as "a man's way of crying." The gender gulf appears to have narrowed, particularly in urban Australia, and a woman's place is now on par with her sisters in other industrialized western societies.

Australia's cultural mix is still evolving, with Britain and the US as the main influences. British visitors notice a California-style informality; American visitors are often surprised by the degree of Britishness remaining. At leisure, young Australians dress like Americans and watch much the same TV shows, but students at private schools continue to wear blazers and boater straw hats like their counterparts in England. Cricket is played on local greens and lawyers appear in court in British-style gowns and horsehair wigs.

Uniting Aussies of all classes, origins, and persuasions is a love of outdoor enjoyment, a passion for sport and a zest for gambling (the latter on anything from horse races to poker machines.) These three pursuits have delighted the citizenry since modern Australia was founded.

FACTS AND FIGURES

Geography: Area 7,682,300 sq km (2,966,136 sq miles), about the size of the continental United States. Nearest neighbors: Indonesia, Papua New Guinea, Solomons, Fiji, and New Zealand. Highest point: Mount Kosciuszko, 2,228 m (7,308 ft); lowest: Lake Eyre, 16 m (52 ft) below sea level.

Population: 19 million in August 1999. One person in four is foreign-born. Approximately 1 percent of the country's population is Aboriginal.

Capital: Canberra (population 309,000)

Major Cities: Sydney (4,041,400), Melbourne (3,417,200), Brisbane (1,601,400), Adelaide (1,092,900), Perth (1,364,200).

Government: Democratic federal constitutional monarchy: Queen Elizabeth II is formally Queen of Australia, represented by a governor-general. Federal government is headed by the prime minister, who is leader of the elected parliamentary majority. Other levels of government: state governments and legislatures, and municipal administrations. There are six states and two mainland territories — the Australian Capital Territory (ACT) and Northern Territory, which has been self-governing since 1978. Voting is compulsory in federal, state, and local elections for everyone except Aborigines, who can choose whether or not to register. If they register, they are obliged to vote.

Economy: Australia is a leading exporter of beef, lamb, wool, wheat, bauxite, nickel, coal, and iron ore. The service sector is the fastest-growing segment of the Australian economy, with tourism the largest and fastest-growing service.

Religion: More than three-quarters of Australians who claim a religion are Christians, mostly Roman Catholics and Anglicans. There are also significant Jewish, Islamic, and Buddhist communities.

Language: English with colorful antipodal embroidery.

A BRIEF HISTORY

The Dreamtime stretches back far longer than many people realize. Australia may have been populated for longer than Western Europe—possibly twice as long. Experts are divided about the dates, with some scientists suggesting that the first inhabitants of Australia arrived 40,000 or 50,000 years ago, and others arguing that it was far earlier.

Dr. Paul Tacon, head of the People and Place Research Center of the Australian Museum, says pollen core samples taken throughout Australia show changes in vegetation and deposition of charcoal "beginning somewhere about 120,000 years ago."

These changes probably resulted from human activity rather than from climatic impact, Dr. Tacon believes.

The first migrations to Australia were most likely spurred by a period of glacial advance that encouraged the shivering cave dwellers of the Northern Hemisphere to head for the sun belt. This move set off a chain reaction, forcing more southerly folk out of their way. As titanic ice caps accumulated, sea levels dropped drastically.

So, in a search for greener pastures or more elbow room, or perhaps blown off course, the original immigrants arrived Down Under by boat from the north. The first Australians had little problem adapting to the new environment. As Stone Age hunters and food gatherers, they were accustomed to foraging, and the takings in the new continent were good: plenty of fish, berries, and roots and, for a change of diet, why not go out and spear a kangaroo?

"The Dreamtime" is the all-purpose name for everything that came before. It puts Aboriginal history, traditions, and culture under a single mythological roof. The Dreamtime's version of Genesis recounts how ancestral heroes created the stars, the earth, and all the creatures. The Dreamtime explains why the animals, insects, and plants are the way they are, and how humans can live in harmony with nature. To this day, when Aboriginal people die, they are recycled to the continuum of the Dreamtime.

Navigators Arrive

For many hundreds of centuries the Aborigines had Australia to themselves. Over the last few hundred years, though, the rest of the world began closing in.

Like the search for El Dorado, everybody seemed to be looking for *Terra Australis Incognita* or "The Great Land of the South." On and off throughout the 16th century, explorers from Europe kept an eye peeled for the legendary continent and its presumed riches.

Some (including the Spanish, Portuguese, and Chinese) may have come close, but the first known landing was by a Dutch captain, Willem Jansz, in 1606. It was a bit of an anticlimax.

"There was no good to be done there," was the conclusion as he weighed anchor. But the merchant adventurers of the Dutch East India Company, the developers of Java, Ceylon, and the Cape of Good Hope, were not to be discouraged. In 1642 the company dispatched one of its ace seafarers, Abel Tasman, to track down the elusive treasures of the farthest continent.

On his first expedition, Tasman discovered an island he called Van Diemen's Land; the modern name honors the finder: Tasmania. A couple of years later Tasman was sent back. He

The Aborigines were the first Australians.

Ancient Aboriginal rock art reveals a finely developed aesthetic sense.

covered much of the coast of northern Australia, but still he found no gold, silver, or spices. Like Jansz before him, Tasman had nothing good to say about the indigenous people, who impressed him as poor, hungry, and generally unattractive brutes. The Dutch named Australia New Holland, but the reports were so unpromising that they never bothered to claim the land.

Another pessimistic view was reported by a colorful traveler, English buccaneer William Dampier, who had two good looks at the west coast of Australia towards the end of the 17th century. He found no drinking water, no fruit or vegetables, no riches, and "the miserablest people in the world."

Botany Bay

Almost by accident, Captain James Cook, the great British navigator, landed on the east coast of Australia in 1770 on a very roundabout trip back to England from Tahiti. Aboard his ship *Endeavour* there were two skilled naturalists, Joseph Banks and Daniel Solander. They found so many fascinating specimens that Cook was moved to name the place Botany Bay.

Cook claimed all the territory he charted for King George III, coining the name New South Wales. He returned to London with glowing reports of the Australia he had seen: a vast, sunny, fertile land, inhabited by a native people who were "far more happier than we Europeans." It was the captain's positive thinking about "noble savages" that was the death of him. A few years later, on the island of Hawaii, he was slain and dismembered by a mob of angry Polynesians.

In 1779, Joseph Banks, who was by now the president of the Royal Society, came up with a novel idea. He formally proposed colonizing Australia, but instead of the conventional type of settlers, he would send out convicts as pioneers. This plan, he contended, would solve the crisis in Britain's overflowing jails. The laws were severe in those days: Even amateur criminals such as petty larcenists, bigamists, and army deserters faced exile.

For most of the 18th century, the British had disposed of troublesome convicts by banishing them to North America. With the American Revolution, though, this desirable destination had to be dropped from the itineraries. The motherland's

In Canberra, a view of the Parliament Building's unusual superstructure.

prisons couldn't possibly cope, and the supplementary river hulks that were used as floating jails threatened riot and disease.

The Banks' proposal for a British version of Devil's Island seemed far-fetched and expensive, but nobody had a better idea, and in May 1787 His Majesty's Government began the transportation of criminals to Australia. The program was to endure for 80 years. During that time more than 160,000 convicts were shipped out to a new life Down Under.

The First Fleet

A retired naval officer, Captain Arthur Phillip, was put in command of the first fleet of 11 sailing vessels carrying nearly 1,500 people—more than half of them convicts—on an eight-month voyage from Portsmouth to New South Wales. Against the odds, the convoy was a success.

Captain Phillip (now titled Governor) came ashore in full ceremonial dress but unarmed. Spear-toting natives milled about like an unwelcoming committee. A lieutenant on the flagship wrote: "I think it is very easy to conceive the ridiculous figure we must appear to these poor creatures, who were perfectly naked."

It also unveiled the truth about Botany Bay: Captain Cook's rosy claims faded to bleak. The expedition's officers were appalled to discover that there was no shelter from east winds, that much of the alleged meadowland was actually swamp, and that there was not enough fresh water to go around.

Luckily, the next best thing to paradise was waiting just around the corner. Governor Phillip, together with a reconnaissance party, sailed 19.5 km (12 miles) up the coast and discovered what Fleet Surgeon John White modestly called "the finest and most extensive harbor in the universe." It could, he reckoned, provide "safe anchorage for all the navies of Europe." It was also strikingly beautiful. Today it's decorated with an Opera House and a bridge and is called Sydney Harbor.

The fleet reassembled at Sydney Cove on 26 January 1788 (the date is recalled every year as the Australian national holiday), and the British flag was raised over the brand-new colony.

On Their Own

London's great expectations took for granted that New South Wales would be instantly self-sufficient. Real life fell dangerously short of the theory. The Sydney summer was too hot for exertions. Even if the convicts had genuinely wanted to pitch in, the soil was unpromising. In any event, most of the outcasts were city-bred and couldn't tell the difference between a hoe and a sickle. Livestock died or disappeared in the bush. Hunger crept into ambush.

Shipwrecks, and delays in London, meant that relief supplies were delayed for nearly two years of increasing desperation. As food supplies dwindled, rations were cut. Prisoners caught stealing food were flogged. Finally, to set an example, the governor ordered a food looter hanged.

In June 1790, to all-round jubilation, the supply ship *Lady Juliana* reached Sydney harbor, and the long fast ended. As agriculture finally began to blossom, many thousands of new prisoners were shipped out. And even voluntary settlers chose Australia as the land of their future.

Enter Captain Bligh

When Governor Phillip retired, the colony's top army officer, Major Francis Grose, took over. His army subordinates fared very well under the new regime, which encouraged free enterprise. The officers soon found profitable sidelines, usually at the expense of the British taxpayers. The army's monopoly on the sale of rum made quick fortunes; under some tipsy economic law, rum began to replace money as Australia's medium of exchange. Even prisoners were paid in alcohol for their extracurricular jobs.

As news of widespread hanky-panky reached London, the government responded by sending out a well-known disciplinarian to shake up the rum-sodden militia. He was Captain William Bligh, target of the notorious mutiny on the *H.M.S. Bounty* seven years earlier. Bligh meant to put fear into the hearts of backsliding officers, but his explosive temper was beyond control. His New South Wales victims nicknamed the new governor Caligula and plotted treason.

Captain Bligh was deposed by a group of insurgent officers on 26 January 1808, as the colony toasted its 20th anniversary. The Rum Rebellion, as the mutiny was dubbed, led to a radical reorganization and reshuffle in personnel. But the inevitable court-martial seemed to understand how Bligh's personality and methods had galled his subordinates. The mutineers were finally punished by more than a rap on the knuckles, but less than they might have expected.

Opening a Continent

New South Wales, under Governor Lachlan Macquarie, overcame the stigma of a penal colony and became a land of opportunity. The idealistic army officer organized the building of schools, a hospital, and a courthouse, as well as roads to link them.

As a method of inspiration for exiles to go straight and win emancipation, Macquarie appointed an ex-convict as Justice of the Peace. Then he invited some of the others to dinner, much to the horror of the local élite. One of the criminals Macquarie pardoned, Francis Greenway, became the colony's prolific official architect.

A field gun displayed at the Australian War Memorial Museum in Canberra.

Some of the ex-convicts fared so well under Macquarie's progressive policies that he was accused of pampering the criminal class. London decreed tougher punishment, along with the total separation of prisoners from the rest of the population. All this led to long-lasting conflict between reformed criminals and their children on one side and a privileged class of immigrants on the other. Nowadays, the shoe is on the other foot: Descendants of First Fleet prisoners often express the same kind of pride as Americans of *Mayflower* ancestry.

The biggest problem for Governor Macquarie and his immediate successors was the colony's position on the edge of the sea. There was not enough land to provide food for the expanding population. The Blue Mountains, which boxed in Sydney Cove, seemed a hopeless barrier. Every attempt to break through the labyrinth of steep valleys failed. Then, in 1813, explorers Blaxland, Wentworth, and Lawson had the unconventional idea of crossing the peaks rather than the vales. It worked. On the far side of the Blue Mountains they discovered a land of plenty, endless plains that would support a great new society.

Other eager adventurers opened new territories. Land was either confiscated or bought from the indigenous tribesmen: For 40,486 hectares (100,000 acres) of what is now Melbourne, the entrepreneurs gave the Aborigines a wagonload of clothing and blankets plus 30 knives, 12 tomahawks, 10 mirrors, 12 pairs of scissors, and 23 kg (50 lbs) of flour. By the middle of the 19th century, thousands of settlers had poured into Australia, and all of the present state capitals were on the map.

Age of Gold

In his understandable enthusiasm, rancher Edward Hargraves slightly overstated the case when he declared: "This is a memorable day in the history of New South Wales. I shall be a baronet." The year was 1851. The place was near Bathurst, about 211 km (130 miles)

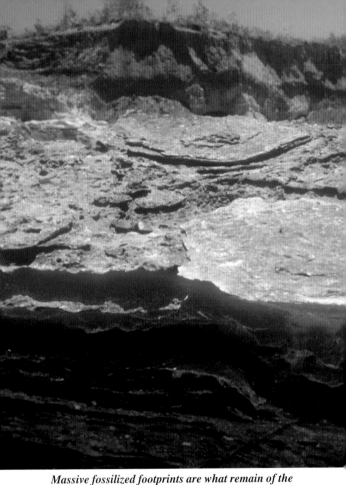

Massive fossilized footprints are what remain of the dinosaurs that once roamed Western Australia.

west of Sydney. Hargraves' audience consisted of one speechless colleague. The occasion was the discovery of gold in Australia.

No sooner had the news of the Bathurst find reached the farthest corner of the land than prospectors from Melbourne struck gold at Ballarat. With two colonies—New South Wales and Victoria—sharing in the boom, adventurers streamed in from both Europe and America. Among them were Australians who had tried to get rich in California's 49er stampede. By the year 1860 Australia's population had reached a total of one million. Thirty-three years later the bonanza became a coast-to-coast celebration when gold was discovered in Kalgoorlie, in Western Australia.

Life in the gold fields was rugged, aggravated by climate, flies, and tax collectors. Whether big winners or, more likely, small losers, all the diggers had to pay the same license fee. Enforcement and fines were needlessly strict. Justice, the miners felt, was tilted against them. So they burned their licenses and demonstrated for voting rights and other reforms. In the subsequent siege of the Eureka Stockade in Ballarat in 1854, troops were ordered to attack the demonstrators. There was heavy loss of life. The license fee was abandoned.

Another riot, in 1861, pitted the white prospectors against Chinese miners, who were resented for their foreignness, strong work ethic, and frugality. At Lambing Flat, New South Wales, thousands of whites whipped and clubbed a community of Chinese. Police, troops, and finally the courts were lenient on the attackers. It was the worst of several race riots. With the tensions of the gold rush, the notion of the "yellow peril" was embedded in Australia's national consciousness.

Rogues on the Range

Transportation of convicts finally ended in 1868, when London had to admit that the threat of exile in Australia was no deterrent to crime.

In Australia itself, crime was always something of a problem; nobody really expected every last sinner to go straight as soon as he arrived. Several wily characters, often escaped convicts, became

Commemorative Courtyard of Canberra's Australian War Memorial Museum, the most visited museum in Australia.

bushrangers, the local version of highwaymen. They occasionally attracted sympathy from Outback folk because they tended to rob the rich and flout authority. As the crimes grew more ambitious or outrageous, their fame was frozen into legend.

The saga of Ned Kelly (1854–1880) reads like Robin Hood gone sour. The Kelly gang preyed on bankers rather than humble ranchers, and Kelly's imaginative operations could be spectacular. But he killed more than his fair share of policemen, almost for the fun of it. Wounded in a shootout, Kelly tried to escape in a suit of homemade armor; this nightmarish contraption deflected most of the bullets, and he was captured wounded but alive. Sentenced to death, he cheekily invited the judge to meet him in the hereafter. Only two weeks after Kelly was hanged, the judge, indeed, died.

An Independent Nation

Having received the blessing of Queen Victoria, the colonies of Australia formed a new nation, the Commonwealth of Australia, on New Year's Day 1901. This federation retained the Queen as head of state, and also bowed to the parliament and Privy Council in London.

Loyalty to the British Empire was tested twice, extravagantly, in the world wars. The Allied defeat at Gallipoli in 1915 was the first and most memorable single disaster for the gallant "diggers," as Australian troops were known. By the end of World War I, more than 200,000 Australians—two-thirds of the entire expeditionary force—had been killed or wounded.

This World War I diorama depicts the brave Australians that served their country during the Great War.

Combat came closer in World War II, when Japanese planes repeatedly bombed Darwin, enemy submarines penetrated Sydney harbor and sank a ferry (the torpedo had been fired at the American warship *USS Chicago*), ships were sunk off the Australian coast and a couple of shells hit Sydney's eastern suburbs. American forces under General Douglas MacArthur arrived in Australia in 1942 and a US force supported by Australia defeated the Japanese decisively in the Battle of the Coral Sea in May of that year. The statistics: 27,000 Australian servicemen died in action on the European and Asian fronts, and nearly 8,000 more died as prisoners of Japan. Almost one in three Australians taken prisoner by the Japanese died in captivity.

After the war, Britain aligned itself with Europe and downgraded its ties with the old Empire. As Britain's regional power declined, Australia boosted its alliance with the United States. Australian troops (over 40,000 of them) fought alongside Americans in Vietnam, sparking vehement anti-war protests in Sydney and other Australian cities. Australian Prime Minister Harold Holt introduced the draft and promised US President Lyndon B. Johnson that Australia would go "all the way with L.B.J." Holt disappeared in 1967 while swimming and may have been eaten by a shark.

The tilt towards the US and Asia showed up also in the trade balance. Before World War II, 42 percent of Australia's overseas trade was with Britain. By 1999, Australia's top 10 export markets included Japan, Korea, Taiwan, China, Singapore, Hong Kong, and Indonesia. Japan buys almost one-fifth of Australia's total merchandise exports. Among non-Asian markets, the most significant for Australian exporters are the United States, New Zealand, and Britain.

Cultural Changes

Another obvious change in orientation is the racial and national background of Australians. Before World War II, 98 percent of the population was of British or Irish birth or descent. As for immigrants, 81 percent of Australia's overseas-born population came from the main

Incredibilities

Who would believe that a creature as odd as the duckbill platypus has been living in Australia since the Ice Age? That so many explorers could come so close and yet miss discovering an island as big as Australia? That the first colonists would be jailbirds? That Captain Bligh, the Bounty tough guy, would be deposed for a second time, in Australia? That California miners would flock to Australia for a replay of the gold rush? That the national song—Waltzing Matilda—would glorify a tea-drinking sheep rustler? Who, indeed?

Mark Twain put it this way: "[Australian history] does not read like history but like the most beautiful lies…. It is full of surprises, and adventures, and incongruities, and contradictions, and incredibilities; but they are all true; they all happened."

English-speaking countries (Britain and Ireland, New Zealand, South Africa, Canada, and the United States.) Since then, the fortress walls of the infamous "White Australia" immigration policy (enacted in 1901 to maintain racial purity) have been torn down under the slogan "Populate or Perish." Australia has seen immigration from many countries including Italy, Greece, the former Yugoslavia, Vietnam, Germany, the Netherlands, the Philippines, Malaysia, Lebanon, Turkey, Hong Kong, China, and South Africa. Australia has accepted more than 470,000 refugees or displaced persons since 1945, creating in the process a culturally diverse nation. About a quarter of Australia's population is overseas-born, a higher proportion than any other country except Israel and Luxembourg. By June 1999, only 39 percent of the overseas-born population had been born in the main English-speaking countries.

Policy towards the Aborigines has softened as well. Aborigines (who make up only about 1 percent of the population) were not permitted to vote in national elections until 1962, and were not included in the census until 1967. Queensland, the final Australian state to grant Aborigines the vote, did so in 1965—almost a century after African-Americans gained the same right following the US Civil War.

In 1990, a government commission gave native peoples the power to make decisions on social and other matters that affect them. In 1993 the government introduced legislation effectively nullifying the doctrine of *terra nullius,* Latin for "empty land." This colonial policy had deemed Australia to be empty at the time of European settlement and thus, by default, the property of the Crown. The court ruling recognized that Aborigines may still hold common law title or "native title" to land.

Support is growing for a treaty with the Aboriginal people to foster national unity. In 2000, in cities throughout Australia, many thousands of citizens marched to demand that the government formally apologize to the Aborigines to begin a process of reconciliation. In Sydney, some 250,000 people marched for the cause.

Fearless But Flawed

He might not have won any popularity contests, but revisionist historians say Captain Bligh really wasn't as bad as he's depicted.

Before his ill-fated career in Australia, Bligh achieved a courageous record. He sailed around the world with Captain Cook, served in naval battles, and revealed his superhuman survival instincts when the Bounty mutineers, preferring Pitcairn Island to home, set him adrift in the Pacific. With fortitude, luck, and exceptional navigating skill, he lived through a voyage of 5,832 km (3,600 miles) in an open boat. By coincidence, Bligh was assigned to suppress a second naval mutiny in 1797, before his appointment to shake up New South Wales.

The short-tempered captain, destined to be portrayed as one of Hollywood's most memorable villains, was eventually promoted to vice admiral.

Moves towards reconciliation intensified from 1991 to 1996 under the enlightened administration of Prime Minister Paul Keating. Keating also argued that Australia should become a republic, engage strongly with Asia, and get rid of Britain's Union Jack flag from the corner of its own flag.

Keating's successor as prime minister, John Howard, is cut from an entirely different political cloth. Howard is an ardent monarchist who has steadfastly refused to apologize to the Aborigines for past wrongs. Howard's main initiative has been to impose a 10 percent tax (GST) on all goods and services. Upon its introduction in 2000, GST raised the cost of many items, including all restaurant meals. Under Howard's stewardship, Australia has concentrated less on Asia and more on traditional alliances in Europe and the US.

Australia severed itself constitutionally from the United Kingdom in 1986. In 1999, there was a referendum held on whether Australia would become a republic. A republic prototype was put to the vote and rejected. Opinion polls before and after the referendum show that Australians do, in fact, favor a republic. The problem was that they disliked the model put forward, which proposed that politicians, rather than the people, should elect the president. Australians have always maintained a healthy disrespect for politicians.

So Australia progressed into the new millennium and the Sydney 2000 Olympic Games, its moment in the world spotlight, with Britain's monarch on its coinage, a governor general as its head of state and the Union Jack adorning its flag.

In 2001, Australia celebrated (in rather low-key fashion) its centenary of federation, when the various British colonies in Australia came together to form one nation. Some year in the future, Australians will again be asked about a republic. Whatever their decision, the 21st century is looking auspicious for the land often termed "The Lucky Country."

WHERE TO GO

Deciding where to go and what to see in Australia may be the hardest part of the journey. How can you cram in so much in a limited time?

About 29 million passengers a year fly Australia's domestic airline routes, and the entry of two new domestic airlines — Virgin Blue and Impulse Airlines — has led to periodic spates of fare discounting. But planning ahead is the best way to ensure low rate airfares. Alternatives are slower, but often more revealing: Try the transcontinental trains and the long-distance buses, some equipped for luxury travel.

Since you probably can't see all of it, you'll have to arrange your tour of Australia to concentrate on touring a manageable slice or two of the continent. Planning your itinerary requires a compromise involving the time and funds you have available, the season, your special interests, and your choice of gateway city. Sydney is the major gateway into Australia, but some fare constructions are flexible and allow you to arrive in Cairns, for example, and depart from Sydney or Perth.

This section of the guide is arranged according to the geographic reality of Australia's states. Although there is no visible difference between the red deserts of the Northern Territory or those of South Australia, it's convenient to consider them in the context of the political frontiers. Besides, the way that history and chance carved Australia into states comes close to providing a fairly natural division into sightseeing regions.

In each state we start with the capital city gateway and fan out from there. We begin where Australia itself began, at Sydney Cove. After a side trip to the federal capital, Canberra, we continue beyond New South Wales, in a counterclockwise direction, from Brisbane in Queensland to Melbourne in Victoria. The section winds up with a look at the continent's lovely green footnote, Tasmania.

NEW SOUTH WALES

Sydney can't help but dominate New South Wales, if only because most of the state's population lives in the capital. But beyond the metropolis, the state — six times the size of England — is as varied as dairyland and desert, as vineyards and craggy mountains.

Sydney

Ever since 1788, when the first convoy of convicts arrived to build a new nation, Sydney's harbor has stolen the show. It is so stunning that people alongside are inspired to achievement and *joie de vivre*.

Australia's oldest, liveliest, and biggest city (total population 4 million) has good reason for self-congratulation. Its 2000 Olympics were acclaimed as the "best Games ever" by International Olympic Committee president Juan Antonio Samaranch. The Games gave Sydney yet another excuse to party — something the city does regularly and fervently, as anyone who has witnessed the annual Sydney Gay and Lesbian Mardi Gras parade (held each March) will affirm. The Mardi Gras brings over 500,000 people onto the streets — by no means all of them gay. It pumps about A$100 million into Sydney's economy, the largest economic impact of any sporting or cultural event in Australia.

If the world had a lifestyle capital, Sydney would be a strong contender (which is richly ironic, considering it started out as a British penal colony). The city is sun-drenched, brawny, energetic, fun-loving, and outdoor-oriented. It ranks highly in world lists of favorite tourist destinations; its residents know this and they revel in it.

After hours — and Sydneysiders do live for the after hours — Sydney offers every imaginable cosmopolitan delight. It's a sunny coincidence that beaches famous for surfing and scenery are only a few minutes away.

Most of the world's great cities have a famous landmark that serves as an instantly recognizable symbol. Sydney has two: the perfect arch of Sydney Harbour Bridge and the billowing roofs of the Sydney Opera House. That's what happens when engineers and architects embellish a harbor coveted by artists as well as admirals.

For a quick appreciation of the intricacies of **Port Jackson** (the official name for Sydney Harbour), gaze out from the top of Sydney Tower at Centrepoint, Sydney's tallest building. See the clear blue tentacles of water stretching from the South Pacific into the heart of the city. Schools of sailing boats vaunt the harbor's perfection in the reflection of the skyscrapers, the classic Sydney Harbour Bridge, and the exhilarating opera house. It's a pity that Captain Cook never noticed this glorious setting as he sailed right past on his way home from Botany Bay.

Most sightseeing tours — by land or sea — leave from Circular Quay (short for Semi-Circular Quay, as it was more accurately named in olden times). Although cruise ships and water taxis alike tie up here, most of the action involves commuter ferryboats and fast "Jetcat" catamarans. The quayside's quota of human interest features hasty travelers, leisurely sightseers, street musicians, artists, and hawkers. Whether you see Australia's busiest harbor from the deck of a luxury liner, a sightseeing boat, or a humble ferry, don't miss this invigorating angle on the city's skyline.

The Rocks

To start at the beginning, stroll through the charming streets of The Rocks, the neighborhood where Sydney was born. You can take a half-hour guided walking tour (adults A$14.85; children A$9.35; Tel. 02 9247 6678) or conduct your own tour. Here modern Australia's founding fathers — convicts who had been charged with anything from shoplifting to major forgery — came ashore in 1788 to build the colony of New South Wales. This historic waterfront district has everything a tourist could want: lovely views at long and short range, moody old buildings, cheerful plazas, and plenty of distractions in the way of shopping, eating, and drinking.

Pick up local leaflets and maps at **The Rocks Visitors' Center,** 106 George Street. You can book tours there as well. This building, too, has a bit of a history. It was built in 1907 as the Coroner's Court.

Cadman's Cottage, next door, is Sydney's oldest (1816) surviving house — a simple stone cottage occupied for many years by the government's official boatsman.

Not far away, the **Museum of Contemporary Art** gives new life to an Art Deco building formerly used by the Maritime Services Board. Few other art museums enjoy such a view! Displays change regularly and the café on the terrace is excellent.

Walking north from Cadman's Cottage past solid old bond stores, now converted to offices and shops such as **Campbell's Storehouse**

The HMAV Bounty, a popular attraction of Sydney's historic district, known as the The Rocks.

(eating, souvenirs, arts and crafts), and you'll arrive at the **Argyle Cut,** a massive excavation hacked with pickaxes through sandstone cliffs by convict labor-gangs. At the top of Argyle Cut, Cumberland Street provides access to Sydney Harbour Bridge via **Cumberland Steps.** In Cumberland Street not far away, the Australian Hotel, a friendly pub in the older Aussie tradition, stocks beers from every state in the country, including a few eagerly sought by connoisseurs. The Australian is one of only two pubs in Sydney to serve unfiltered beers created by master brewer Geoff Scharer. They are acclaimed by expert tasters and seasoned journalists as possibly the best beers in Australia.

A little further on, in Argyle Place, you will find a neat row of terraced houses straight out of Georgian England. Two other grand old pubs in this area deserve mention. The quaint **Hero of Waterloo** at 81 Lower Fort Street was built in 1843 on top of a maze of subterranean cellars through which drunken patrons were conveyed to be sold as crew to unscrupulous sea captains. That practice has died out but the cellars remain.

The Lord Nelson, a square sandstone block of a building at the corner of Kent and Argyle Street, was built about 1840 and has maintained a British naval atmosphere ever since. It brews its own beers, some of them pretty strong.

For history without the refreshments, visit the Garrison Church, officially named the **Holy Trinity Anglican Church,** which dates from the early 1840s. As the unofficial name indicates, it was the church for members of the garrison regiment, the men in charge of the convict colony. It's now a fashionable place to get married.

At the start of George Street, close to the Irish-influenced Mercantile Hotel, **The Rocks Market** takes place each Saturday and Sunday, under a 150-m-long (492-ft) canopy. Musical groups and street entertainers perform, while stall-holders sell crafts, leatherwear, souvenirs, toys, and gifts. Not far away, Customs Officers Stairs lead down to some charming harborside restaurants housed in old bond stores, fronting **Campbells Cove.**

Here, you're in the shadow of **Sydney Harbour Bridge,** with its drive-through stone pylons (purely ornamental) and colossal steel arch. The bridge stars on television each New Year's Eve, when it serves as a platform for a spectacular fireworks display. To bid farewell to 1999 and welcome in 2000, hundreds of fireworks were fired from the arch in a spectacular computer-controlled sequence. Other fireworks positioned on the road-span created a Niagara-like cascade into Sydney Harbour, while the bridge lit up with the word "Eternity" — (the word scrawled in chalk on Sydney sidewalks for nearly 40 years by a reformed petty criminal who died in 1967).

Linking the city and the north, the bridge's single arch is 503 m (1,650 ft) across, and wide enough to carry eight lanes of cars and two railway tracks, as well as lanes for pedestrians and cyclists. When it was built, during the Great Depression, Sydneysiders called the bridge the Iron Lung, because it kept a lot of people "breathing" — in economic terms. It takes ten years to repaint the bridge, at the end of which time it's time to start again. To ease traffic congestion a tunnel has also been built under the harbor.

An unusual vantage point for viewing the bridge, the harbor, and the skyline is from the top of one of the bridge's massive pylons. The **lookout** is in the southeast tower, and the stairway can be reached via Cumberland Street, The Rocks. It's open every day of the year, except for Christmas Day.

A company called BridgeClimb conducts guided walks for small groups over the bridge's massive arches. Not across the walkway below, but over the arches above. For decades, groups of daredevils have been doing this illicitly. Since the legal climb began in 1998 the waiting list has grown quite long and it pays to book your climb as far in advance as you can. You can even do the climb at night, though climbs are postponed during electrical storms (good thinking!). It's not a cheap thrill — expect to pay about A$100; Tel. (02) 9252 0077.

City Center

Sydney Tower at Centrepoint is the city's highest vantage point — at 305 m (1,001 ft) above the street. It takes only 40 seconds to reach the observation decks (and the revolving restaurant invariably found at such altitudes). Amateur photographers get that glazed look as they peer through the tinted windows to unlimited horizons. On a flawless day you can see all the way north to Terrigal and south to Wollongong, far out to sea, or as far west as the Blue Mountains. Otherwise, look out and down at the seething shopping streets all around the tower.

One of the streets below is the city's main square, **Martin Place,** flanked by the imposing Victorian Renaissance-style **General Post**

Sydney's Harbour Bridge filters the light at sunset.

Office (GPO) building. This has been imaginatively converted into a stylish modern complex including a 418-room, five-star Westin hotel. The ornate GPO façade has been retained. During World War II, the GPO's clock tower was dismantled for fear that Japanese bombers might zero in on the landmark. The clock was restored 20 years later.

From the same era as the GPO, but even grander, the **Queen Victoria Building** (QVB) occupies an entire block on George Street (Sydney's main street and the oldest street in Australia) opposite Sydney Town Hall. The Byzantine-style QVB began as a municipal market and commercial center, including a hotel and a concert hall, topped by statuary and 21 domes. Built in 1898 to commemorate Queen Victoria's Golden Jubilee, it was condemned to demolition in the 1960s by small-minded officials to make way for a parking garage. Fortunately, the authorities ran short of money, the demolition was put on hold and the building was faithfully restored in the 1980s to create a magnificent all-weather shopping center housing nearly 200 chic boutiques, cafés and restaurants, in a cool and unhurried atmosphere of period charm. Pierre Cardin called it "the most beautiful shopping center in the world."

Next door, Sydney's **Town Hall** enlivens a site that used to be a cemetery. The Victorian building, home of the city council, is also used for concerts and exhibitions. **St. Andrew's Cathedral** next door, Anglican and newly renovated, is the oldest cathedral in Australia.

Chinatown

After dark, young Sydneysiders flock to the section of George Street heading south from the Town Hall, lined with video enter- tainment arcades, fast-food joints, and a movie complex. Sydney's fledgling Latin Quarter begins nearby on the corner of George Street and Liverpool Street — there's a choice of *tapas* bars here. In the adjacent Chinatown district, gourmets enjoy the delights of Peking, Cantonese, and Szechuan cuisine. The large local Chinese community is joined by Sydneysiders and tourists enjoying the Chinese cafés, restaurants, and shops selling exotic spices and knickknacks. The district's centerpiece is **Dixon Street,** a pedestrian zone framed by ceremonial gates. If you're here at the weekend, check out **Paddy's Market,** a cavernous brick building beneath a new skyscraper. Paddy's is full of stalls selling almost anything: souvenirs, seashells, sunglasses, fruit, vegetables, and semi-antiques. On level three of the same complex you'll find **Kam Fook** Shark's Fin Seafood Restaurant, a Chinese eatery of such enormity waiters use mobile phones to converse with the kitchen.

Darling Harbour, nearby, is well-stocked with shops, restaurants, and attractions. A **monorail** system links it to more central areas. On the city side of Darling Harbour is **Cockle Bay,** a complex of bars and restaurants. This has proved much more popular than the harborside shopping and dining complex on the western side, mainly because Cockle Bay is easier to reach on foot from downtown Sydney.

Not far away, **Sydney Aquarium** is one of the largest aquariums in the world. In the Open Ocean Oceanarium there, large sharks weigh up to 300 kg (660 pounds) and measure over 9 m (30 ft) long. The Great Barrier Reef Complex there houses over 6,000 creatures, and a visit there is the closest thing to diving on the reef without getting wet.

Other nearby attractions include the **Sydney Maritime Museum** and the **Sydney Entertainment Centre,** the latter used for sports events and concerts.

The Parks

Sydney's lush Hyde Park is only a fraction the size of its namesake in London, but it provides the same sort of green relief. And like most big-city parks, it should be avoided after sunset. The most formal feature of the semi-formal gardens, the **Anzac War Memorial,** commemorates the World War I fighters in monumental Art-Deco style, with later acknowledgements to the World War II contingent.

Sightseers interested in old churches should mark a few targets on the edge of Hyde Park. To the north, the early colonial **St. James' Church** in Queens Square was the work of the convict architect, Francis Greenway. Just across College Street on the east, **St. Mary's Cathedral** stands on the prominent site of the colony's first Catholic church. The sandstone spires at the southern end are new. While included in the original plan in 1865, the spires were not added until just before the 2000 Olympics. That's why they are somewhat lighter in color.

You can view the spires while immersed in a swimming pool next door at **Cook and Phillip Park.** This aquatic, fitness, and recreation center opened in 1999. You can't readily see the complex from the street, yet when you're inside its huge windows give views and let in plenty of light. There are three pools — one with a wave machine. A swim here costs A$4.50 for adults and A$3.30 for children, or A$11 if you want to use the well-equipped gym as well. There's a café inside, or if you want to eat alfresco, Bodhi's vegan restaurant does good business just outside.

The ornate **Great Synagogue** faces the park across Elizabeth Street. Jews have lived in Sydney since the arrival of the first shipment of prisoners.

The **Australian Museum,** on College Street, specializes in natural history and anthropology. On the second floor in a glass tank, you may even find a couple of live specimens of the world's largest cockroach. The giant burrowing cockroach (*Macropanesthia rhinoceros*) is native to Australia. It feeds on dead eucalyptus leaves and dwells in woodland, growing up to 10 cm (4 inches) long and weighing up to almost 50 grams (1.75 ounces) — or about the weight of an AA-size battery. Don't miss the "Bone Ranger" skeleton display or the big Museum Shop downstairs.

The restored **Hyde Park Barracks** (designed by Greenway), is now a museum of social history, located between Hyde Park and the Botanic Gardens. On the top floor of the barracks, one large room is a reconstruction of the dormitory life of the prisoners. **The Mint,** next door, processed gold-rush bullion in the mid-19th century.

Another large park adjacent to Hyde Park is called **The Domain**. For a century or so, it has contained the local equivalent of London's Hyde Park Corner, where anyone can climb aboard a soapbox and make a speech; Sunday is the day of the orators and hecklers. The **Art Gallery of New South Wales** there consists of a formal exterior decorated with much bronze statuary and a modern extension, added in 1988, which infuses light into the building and provides sweeping views of east Sydney, part of the harbor, and the suburb of **Woolloomooloo.**

An afternoon at the Art Gallery will give you a crash course in more than a century of traditional and modern Australian art. The **Yiribana Gallery** there is devoted to Aboriginal art and Torres Islander art.

Sydney's **Royal Botanic Gardens** began as a different sort of garden: Here the early colonists tried — with very limited success — to grow vegetables. Only a few steps from the busy skyscraper world of downtown Sydney, you can relax in the shade of Moreton Bay fig trees, palms, or mighty mahoganies, or enter a glass pyramid full of orchids and other tropical beauties. The gardens curve up around Farm Cove to a peninsula with the quaint name of **Mrs. Macquarie's Point.** The lady thus immortalized, the wife of the go-ahead governor, used to admire the view from here; now it's better than ever.

Centennial Park, best reached from the eastern end of Oxford Street in the inner-city suburb of **Paddington,** has provided greenery and fresh air to city folk since 1888, when it was dedicated on the centenary of Australia's foundation to "the enjoyment of the people of New South Wales forever."

Centennial Park's 220 hectares (544 acres) of trees, lawns, duck ponds, rose gardens, and bridle-paths are visited by about three million people a year, who cycle, roller-blade, walk their dogs, feed birds, play team sports, throw frisbees, fly kites, picnic, and barbecue seafood or sausages.

Centennial Park, and **Lachlan Swamp** within it, supports large numbers of birds. Species include distinctive long-beaked ibises, which look like something off the wall of an ancient Egyptian tomb but are, in fact, native to Australia. Flocks of loud-squawking sulfur-crested cockatoos make their presence known.

Bats twitter in the park's venerable Moreton Bay fig trees and possums (the native Australian type) dwell in the date palms. The palms themselves are under threat from a mysterious virus and are being progressively replaced with more resistant species.

If you fancy a ride on the bridle path, horse rental can be arranged from Moore Park Stables, Tel. (02) 9360 8747. Bicycles and pedal-carts can be hired from Centennial Park Cycles, Tel. (02) 9398 5027.

Centennial Park Kiosk, a lovely setting for a meal and a glass of wine, was renovated and expanded in 1998. Beside it stands a charming, if curious, modern stone fountain.

Centennial Park Amphitheater provides an outdoor venue for events and productions. In the summer months, a popular Moonlight Cinema program is held in the amphitheater. Films start at about 8:45pm and tickets are available at the gate from 7:30pm. For screening details, Tel. 1900 933 899.

Sydney Opera House

There's a real sense of occasion and style about the familiar structure of the Sydney Opera House, both inside and out. This one-in-a-million building, covered in a million tiles, has achieved the seemingly impossible and improved a virtually perfect harbor. Yet its controversial architect left the country in a huff at an early stage of construction.

Close-up of Sydney Opera House, showing off its uniquely spherical construction.

Until the opera house idea was underway, the promontory was wasted on a fancy, turreted depot for tramcars. In the 1950s the government of New South Wales decided to build a performing arts center there. A Danish architect, Jørn Utzon, won an international competition to design it. His novel plan included problems of spherical geometry so tricky that he actually chopped up a wooden sphere to prove it could be done.

The inspiring shell of the complex was virtually complete when Utzon walked out, and the interior, which was in dispute, became the work of a committee. Despite this, from the tip of its highest roof (67 m/220 ft above sea level), to the Drama Theater's orchestra pit (more than a fathom *below* sea level), this place has grace, taste, and class.

The name "Sydney Opera House" is as renowned worldwide as it is inaccurate. The actual opera theater is only one of the center's five, and it is not the biggest. (Incidentally, if you're "fashionably late" for the opera, there is no admission until the first intermission, probably the end of the first act — and that goes for VIPs as well as tourists.) It's worth taking a guided tour of the whole building. Tours depart about every 30 minutes from 9:15am to 4pm each day, except for Christmas Day and Good Friday.

Kings Cross

East of The Domain lies the district of Woolloomooloo (the nifty name has something to do with kangaroos in an Aboriginal language). A spelling teaser for Australian school children, Woolloomooloo was threatened by wholesale demolition in the 1970s, but was saved by resident protests and union "green bans."

East of Woolloomooloo, bright lights and shady characters exist side by side in Kings Cross, a couple of railway stops from circular

Sydney Opera House at night, renowned the world over for its bold organic design.

Quay. "The Cross," as it's often called, is Sydney's version of Paris's Pigalle or London's Soho — neon-filled, a bit tacky but rather fun, crawling with hedonists of all persuasions. Action continues 24 hours a day, with a diverting cavalcade of humanity — the brightly colored, the bizarre, the grotesque, the stoned, the happy and the drunk. On weekends, tourists flock to the Cross to glimpse a bit of weirdness. Sometimes though, the weirdest characters they spot are other tourists.

The Cross's "main drag" (major street) is **Darlinghurst Road,** bohemian verging on sleazy and dotted with a jumble of bars, strip joints, fast-food outlets, tattoo parlors and X-rated book and video shops. The **Bourbon and Beefsteak Bar** is a fun place for a few drinks, if rather touristy these days. It was highly popular with American servicemen on R&R leave in the 1960s during the Vietnam War.

Kings Cross is famous (or infamous) for its "spruikers" (pronounced sprookers) — fast-talking salesmen who hang around the doors of strip clubs and try to lure passers-by inside. Predictably, their main targets are single men or men in groups. They tend to leave mixed-sex couples or mixed-sex groups alone.

Kings Cross also offers reputable hotels and shops, a fountain commemorating the World War II desert battle of El Alamein, and good ethnic restaurants.

A five-minute walk from Kings Cross Station brings you to **Elizabeth Bay House,** a stately home built in 1835 and a reminder that the Kings Cross precinct was once highly respectable.

If you have time for one more inner suburb, make it **Paddington,** to the southeast of Kings Cross. Its trademark is the intricate wrought-ironwork, known as Sydney Lace, on the balconies of 19th-century terraced houses. This feature, and the rather bohemian atmosphere, reminds some travelers of New Orleans. After decades of dilapidation, the district came up in the world rapidly as a fashionable, rather artsy place to live. It has developed into one of

Sydney's most sought-after suburbs, with house prices to match. "Paddo," as the locals like to call it, offers plenty of ethnic restaurants, antiques shops, art galleries, fashionable bookshops, and trendy boutiques. One of Sydney's best public markets, **Paddington Bazaar,** is held each Saturday on the grounds of Paddington Public School in Oxford Street. It offers every type of art and craft and is enlivened by a variety of street entertainers.

Paddington's main street, Oxford Street is a center for Sydney's large gay community, with the Albury the street's longest-established gay pub. The Street is home to two of Sydney's best bookshops, Ariel and Berkelouw, and three of its more imaginative cinemas, the Chauvel, the Verona, and the Academy Twin.

Victoria Barracks is Oxford Street's renowned example of mid-19th-century military architecture, built by convicts to house a regiment of British soldiers and their families.

Around Sydney Harbor

Take a harbor cruise to appreciate hidden beaches, islets, mansions old and new, even a couple of unsung bridges. Various companies run half-day and full-day excursions. Or you can rent a boat of your own in which to weave around the nautical traffic.

Among the harbor highlights: **Fort Denison,** situated on a small island, is graphically nicknamed "Pinchgut." Before the construction of a proper prison, the colony's more troublesome convicts were banished to the rock to subsist on a bread-and-water diet. In the middle of the 19th century the island was fortified to guard Sydney from the far-fetched threat of a Russian military strike. Ironically, the only attack came in World War II when an American warship, conducting target practice, hit old Pinchgut by mistake.

Taronga Zoo, a 12-minute ferry ride from Circular Quay, boasts a superb setting. Over the heads of the giraffes you can see across the harbor to the skyscrapers of Sydney. The zoo's Nocturnal House features indigenous night-time creatures illuminated in artificial

Undaunted by the occasional shark, surfers flock to Sydney's famed Bondi beach.

moonlight, unaware of onlookers. The Rainforest Aviary houses hundreds of tropical birds. If you arrange your visit around feeding times, which are posted at the gate, you can watch the keepers distribute food while they deliver talks about their charges.

Vaucluse House, a stately home with its own beach, adds its mock-Gothic turrets and battlements to the skyline. The splendid, 15-room mansion, begun in 1803, is run by the state's Historic Houses Trust. It's also reachable by bus or taxi.

Farther afield, both north and south of Sydney, are miles of inviting beaches. **Manly** got its name when the first governor of the colony thought the Aborigines sunning themselves on the beach looked manly. This pleasant north-shore resort has beaches back to back, linked by the lively Corso — a promenade full of restaurants and tables for picnickers.

Bondi, pronounced *bond-eye,* is a favorite with surfers and an Australian icon. The varied characters on the sand range from ancient sunworshippers to bathing beauties. Note that if a warning bell clangs on the beach, it signifies a shark alert; perhaps a false one, but don't assume so.

Bondi's main promenade, Campbell Parade, is lined with dozens of restaurants and one pub, the **Bondi Hotel,** open until 4am six days a week and until midnight on Sundays.

Olympic Sydney

The Sydney 2000 Olympic and Paralympic Games are history but the euphoria lingers and Sydneysiders fondly remember their city's moment in the limelight. Athletes coined the phrase "the Games of Smiles." Observers from around the world remarked how Australians cheered spontaneously for all teams and competitors, not just their own side. After US sprint star Marion Jones won her three gold medals, Marion's mother (who visited Sydney with her family for the Games), was moved to write to the *Sydney Morning Herald* to thank Aussie fans who, even when Marion beat Australian contenders, "applauded Marion at the end, respected her, afforded her the dignity and the courtesy which I have never seen anywhere else. Thank you Australia, and thanks for loving my daughter Marion."

Now the Games are over, Sydney's magnificent, purpose-built Olympic Park is somewhat under-employed. Critics speak of a white elephant, and say it will be at least a decade before the facility becomes self-sufficient and able to cover its costs. Other cities have encountered similar post-Games challenges.

The Park is still fun to visit and you can swim at the excellent **Aquatic Center.** Allow a full day if you want to visit each venue at the site; otherwise, half a day is probably enough. The best way to get there is to catch a Parramatta Rivercat ferry from Circular Quay. These depart hourly and give a 50-minute scenic river trip before you alight at Homebush and catch an Olympic Explorer bus. Buses depart every 20 minutes. You can hop on and off as you please all day. On weekdays, the Rivercat Olympic Explorer Combined Ticket costs A$20 round-trip for adults and A$10 for children. (Tel: 131 500.) Guided walking tours and cycling tours of Olympic venues are available. If you want an in-depth tour, Stadium Australia tours are A$26 for adults, A$19.50 for students and

Stadium Australia, parabolic centerpiece of Sydney's Olympic Park, built for the 2000 games.

seniors, A\$13 for children 5–16. Explorer bus passengers are entitled to discounted prices of A\$21 for adults; A\$10.50 for children. (Tel. 02 8765 2300.)

Stadium Australia

The graceful, parabola-shaped centerpiece of Olympic Park, Stadium Australia was Sydney's premier Olympic venue, hosting the Opening and Closing Ceremonies, the track and field program and the closing stages of the Marathon. The Stadium is the largest ever built for Olympic Games.

Millennium Parklands

A giant new park called Millennium Parklands has been created from 450 hectares (1,112 acres) of landscape around the Olympic facilities and the new Sydney Showground which adjoins it. Bigger than New York's Central Park and twice the size of Sydney's pre-existing Centennial Park, Millennium Parklands was one of very few large parks to open within a major world city in the 20th century.

Before the park and the Olympic facilities could be built, a massive clean-up of the site was required. It had previously served as a saltworks, a brickworks, an abattoir, a naval armaments depot and a landfill dump. Native foliage has been replanted and a more natural creek system recreated, with meandering pools to encourage wildlife to return. Studies show birds and fish are coming back, including a regular visitor to Homebush Bay, the Golden Plover, which flies a 22,000-km (13,670-mile) round trip to Australia from Alaska each year.

Olympic Village

"The world's most environmentally friendly village", a short walk from Stadium Australia, was built to house the athletes. It's now one of Sydney's newest environs, billed as the world's largest

The Three Sisters, dramatic geology of the world-renowned Blue Mountains, 90 minutes west of Sydney.

solar-powered suburb, with the capacity to generate more than 1 million kilowatt-hours of power annually.

Aquatic Paradise

The Sydney International Aquatic Centre (SIAC) welcomes athletes, community groups, overseas visitors, and families for watersports, recreational swimming, carnivals, and fun. This was not built specifically for the Games, but it was certainly in the right place! Four pools include a leisure pool, complete with palm trees and colorful mosaics, encompassing five spas, a river ride, spray jets, spurting 'volcanoes', a water slide, and bubble beach. Children love it, as do serious swimmers.

Super Showground

Sydney Showground, next to the main Olympic site, attracted 1.2 million people to the first Royal Easter Show held there in 1998. The Showground's environmentally passive, ingeniously designed halls and pavilions minimize the need for air-conditioning and heating.

Excursions

Within day-trip distance of Sydney — by car, train, or sightseeing bus — a choice of scene-changers shows the big variety of attractions offered by New South Wales. Any of the most popular outings will deepen your understanding of Australia and its assets.

Blue Mountains

A 90-minute trip to the west of Sydney by road brings you to the Blue Mountains, a scenically dramatic region of forested ravines and pristine bushland that recently gained a World Heritage listing.

As well as its scenic and environmental value, the Blue Mountains offer a wealth of adventure activities, art and craft galleries, and romantic escapes in grand country lodges or cozy bed and breakfasts.

Sublime Point, Blue Mountains — the blue haze comes from evaporating eucalyptus oil from the millions of gum trees.

The name "Blue Mountains" derives from the mountains' distinctive blue haze, produced by eucalyptus oil evaporating from millions of gum trees. Well-marked walking trails criss-cross Blue Mountains National Park, passing streams and waterfalls, descending into cool gorges, and snaking around sheer cliffs.

This breathtaking environment is easily reached from Sydney, either by road or on a two-hour rail journey. Trains run there several times daily from Central Station.

The region's best-known rock formation is **The Three Sisters,** a trio of pinnacles best viewed from **Katoomba,** the largest of 26 mountain towns. **Katoomba Scenic Rail,** the world's steepest railway, descends from the cliff-top at Katoomba down into the Jamison Valley. You can walk down a series of steps by The Three Sisters, stroll along a cool and refreshing trail and catch the Katoomba Scenic Rail to the top. Above, the **Skyway** carries passengers along a cableway 206 m (675 ft) above the valley floor.

Katoomba's **Maxvision** giant screen is a relatively recent Blue Mountains innovation. It shows *The Edge — The Movie,* a gripping presentation of Blue Mountains environment, history, and ecology. You'll learn about the Wollemi Pine, the world's oldest species of tree.

Unique to the Blue Mountains, this ancient genus of pine was discovered in 1994 by the New South Wales National Parks and Wildlife Service. The tree's closest relations became extinct during the Jurassic and Cretaceous periods between 65 to 200 million years ago.

As one Sydney-based botanist exclaimed at the time: "This is like finding a living dinosaur in your backyard!"

For more than a century, spelunkers, hikers, and ordinary tourists have admired the **Jenolan Caves,** at the end of a long, steep drive down the mountains from Katoomba. Guided tours through the spooky but often awesome limestone caverns last about an hour and a half. The atmosphere is cool in summer, warm in winter, and always damp.

Old Sydney Town

North of Sydney, beyond the sparkling waters of the Hawkesbury River, history buffs can visit a reconstruction of the original penal colony, Old Sydney Town. Here budding actors in period costumes duel, march, fire musket and cannon, flog convicts, and generally keep themselves busy amusing and informing visitors. It's a hugely entertaining and educational day out. The best idea is to arrive at about 10am and follow the action around. If you get bored you can always go next door and spend the rest of the day at the **Australian Reptile Park.**

On the way to Old Sydney Town, the Pacific Highway cuts through Ku-ring-gai Chase National Park. This compact area of unspoiled forests, cliffs, and heathland is home base for numerous species of animals and birds. But you have to find them for yourself; it's not a zoo. The Aborigines who lived in this area long before the foundation of New South Wales left hundreds of rock carvings—pictures of animals and supernatural beings. The park information center has maps pinpointing the location of the most interesting of the carvings.

Hunter Valley

Australia is one of the world's major wine-producing countries. The Hunter Valley is the premier wine-growing area of New South Wales, a two-hour drive from Sydney. The Hunter's 50 wineries harvest grapes in February and March and welcome visitors throughout the year. Gateway to the Pokolbin region—where most of the Lower Hunter Valley wineries are located—is Cessnock, 195 km (121 miles) north of Sydney, where the local tourist information center supplies touring maps and brochures.

Most of the Hunter wineries are open for cellar-door tastings. Some of the major wineries include Tyrell's Wines, Lindemans Winery, Wyndham Estate, the Hunter Estate, Rothbury Estate, and the McWilliams Mount Pleasant Winery.

Newcastle, commercial center of The Hunter, is located about 170 km (106 miles) north of Sydney. It's a coalmining and ship-building center which also offers well-developed recreational possibilities on the Pacific, the **Hunter River,** and the saltwater **Lake Macquarie.** The lake, popular with weekend sailors and fishermen from far afield, is said to be the largest seaboard lake in Australia.

Further north, **Port Stephens** offers safe swimming beaches, a range of water activities and good fishing. Its bay is home to dozens of bottlenose dolphins, which can be viewed up close on a cruise.

In the far north of New South Wales, **Byron Bay** provides wonderful beaches and great surf. It's a haven for alternative lifestylers — a few of them very rich.

Lord Howe Island

In the South Pacific, 483 km (299 miles) east of Port Macquarie, Lord Howe Island, the state's off-shore possession, is said to be the world's most southerly coral isle. This makes for splendid snorkeling and scuba diving. Lord Howe Island has been on the UNESCO World Heritage list since 1982. If you prefer to stay dry you can go out in a glass-bottom boat. Forests, beaches, mountains and all, Lord Howe Island only amounts to a speck in the ocean—1,305 hectares (3,223 acres)—so bicycles and motorbikes are ideal for getting around.

You can fly out from Sydney to this sleepy lagoon in a couple of hours.

Snowy Mountains

If you've come to Australia in search of snow, you need go no farther than the southeastern corner of New South Wales. Skiing in the Snowy Mountains is usually restricted to the months of July, August, and September. But even in the antipodean summer a few drifts of snow remain to frame the wild flowers of the Australian Alps. At the top of this world is Mount Kosciuszko, at 2,228 m (7,308 ft) high, named after an 18th-century Polish patriot by a 19th-century Polish explorer. This is the birthplace of three important rivers, the Murray, the Murrumbidgee, and the Snowy.

Kosciuszko National Park is made up of about 6,300 sq km (2,432 sq miles) of the kind of wilderness you won't see anywhere else: buttercups and eucalyptus and snow, all together in the same breathtaking panorama. The only thing missing is a pine tree, or any of the other familiar conifers of the Northern Hemisphere.

Cars must be equipped with snow chains from 1 June to 10 October. However, even in summer the weather can change for the worse at very short notice, so be sure to always carry a warm, waterproof jacket. The best-known ski resorts in this area are **Thredbo** and **Perisher Valley**.

N.S.W. Outback

Although New South Wales is the most populous and productive state (in both manufacturing and farming), it extends to infinities of Australian Outback — bushland and cattle stations seem thousands of miles from commuterland.

Dubbo is the sort of place where the Old Gaol (jail), meticulously restored, is a prime tourist attraction, gallows and all. Just out of town, the Western Plains Zoo is advertised as Australia's only open-range zoo, a cageless convention of koalas, dingoes, and emus, plus more exotic (to Australians) animals like giraffes, zebras, and monkeys.

Lightning Ridge, in the Back of Beyond near the Queensland border, enjoys one of the most evocative of Outback names. Fortune hunters know it well as the home — reputedly the only home — of the precious black opal. Tourists are treated to demonstrations of fossicking, and there are opportunities to shop for opals.

Bourke is a small town whose name signifies the loneliness of the Outback, where dusty tracks are the only link between distant hamlets. "Back of Bourke" is an Australian expression for *really* far-out Outback. Bourke looks a lot bigger on the map than on the ground.

Broken Hill (population more than 23,300) is about as far west as you can go in New South Wales, and is situated almost on the border with South Australia. It's so far to the west of Sydney there's a half-hour time difference, even though both are in the same state. The town is legendary for its mineral wealth — it has produced millions of tons of silver, lead, and zinc. Tourists can visit the mines, either underground or on the top. The neatly laid-out town, with its streets named after various minerals — Iodide, Kaolin, Talc — has become an artistic center, with works by Outback painters on show in numerous galleries. Pro Hart, one of Australia's best-known and most prolific painters, is a long-time Broken Hill resident.

CANBERRA

Australia, the lucky country, lived up to its reputation when it came to picking the site for a national capital. Out of conflict emerged a green and pleasant compromise, far from the pressures of the big cities. Where sheep had grazed, the young Commonwealth raised its flag.

When the new nation was proclaimed at the turn of the 20th century, the perennial power struggle between Sydney and Melbourne reached an awkward deadlock. Each of the cities offset its rival's claim to be the national capital. So they carved out a site in the rolling bush 320 km (198 miles) southwest of Sydney, and it soon began to sprout clean white official buildings, followed by millions of trees and shrubs. As compromises go, it was a winner.

To design a model capital from scratch, the way Washington, D.C. or St. Petersburg, Russia, were laid out, Australia opened an

Lake Burley Griffin, Canberra, with its famous water jet honoring Captain Cook.

international competition. The prize was awarded to an American architect, Walter Burley Griffin. He did, indeed, have a grand design. But it took longer than anyone imagined to transfer his plan from the drawing board to reality, owing not only to the distractions of two world wars and the Depression, but also to a great deal of wrangling. Burley Griffin, a Chicagoan of the Frank Lloyd Wright school, put great emphasis on coherent connections between the settings and the buildings, and between landscape and cityscape. He never visited the site and he died 20 years before his city could prove itself.

Canberra's name, which is said to be derived from "meeting place" in an Aboriginal tongue, was officially chosen in 1913 from among a huge outpouring of suggestions. Some of the more serious people wanted to have a name as uplifting as Utopia or Shakespeare. Others devised classical constructions like Auralia and Austropolis. The most unusual proposal was a coinage designed to soothe every state capital: Sydmeladperbrisho. And after that mouthful, the name Canberra came as a relief.

At the heart of the Australian Capital Territory, Canberra has a population of about 309,000. Although the city is an educational and research center, it's essentially a company town; the local industry is government. The ministries are here, and the parliament with its politicians, lobbyists, and hangers-on, and the foreign embassies to add their exotic contribution. In spite of this considerable enterprise, Australia's only sizeable inland city is uncrowded and relaxed. The Royal Military College Duntroon, Australia's first military college, founded in 1911, is based here. Tours of the grounds start in Starkey Park, Jubilee Avenue, on weekends. Also in Canberra is the Australian Institute of Sport, which offers public tours, a shop selling AIOS merchandise, and a café.

City Sights

There are several good ways to see Canberra, but not on foot. Pedestrians are out of luck in the great expanses of this city of parks.

Australian War Memorial Museum (foreground) at the head of the ceremonial avenue known as ANZAC Parade.

As on any map of Australia, the distances are greater than you think. If you do want to walk, many of the main attractions are found near Lake Burley Griffin — but you'll still need three or four hours. It's a good idea to sign up for a bus tour; they come in half-day and all-day versions. Or take Murray's Explorer bus, which runs a 25 km route stopping at all the main sights. You buy an all-day ticket, then hop on and off at will. Or you can drive yourself around the town, following itineraries mapped out in a free sightseeing pamphlet. Motorists arriving from either Sydney or Melbourne can pick this leaflet up, along with other leaflets, maps, and advice, on the way into Canberra at the Canberra Visitors Center, Northbourne Avenue, Dickson; Tel. (02) 6205 0044. In the middle of town, Travelers Maps and Guides is located in the Jolimont Center, Northbourne Avenue; Tel. (02) 6249 6006.

An effective starting place for a do-it-yourself tour of Canberra is **Regatta Point,** which overlooks the lake that Burley Griffin cleverly created in the middle of town.

Man-made **Lake Burley Griffin,** 35 km (22 miles) around, is generously named after the town planner who realized the value of water for recreation as well as scenic beauty. Currently you can enjoy fishing, sailing, and windsurfing here, although plans for sightseeing boats are in the works. Whooshing up from the lake, a giant **water jet** honors the explorer Captain Cook for several hours each day (10am–noon and 2pm–4pm — plus 7pm–9pm during summer). The **Carillon,** another monument rising from Lake Burley Griffin (actually from a small island), was a gift from the British government. Apart from concert recitals, it tells the time every 15 minutes, taking its tune from London's Big Ben.

North of the Lake

Canberra is older and greener than Brasília, and is harder to navigate around than an earlier "artificial" capital, Washington DC. To get the big picture, have a look at the view from the **Telstra Tower** atop **Black Mountain.** Millions of sightseers have paid to ascend the 195-m (640-ft) tower for the 360° perspective. With Canberra's pollution-free atmosphere, it's usually worth the investment, even at night, when the capital's public buildings are illuminated. A viewing platform circles the structure towards the top. And the designers couldn't resist adding a café and a revolving restaurant. If you want to eat there, you'll have to book ahead — Tel. (02) 6248 6162.

On the eastern slopes of Black Mountain, the **National Botanic Gardens** are entirely devoted to Australian flora — they boast the most comprehensive collection anywhere. In spite of Canberra's mostly mild, dry climate, numerous rainforest specimens flourish under intensive care. Walter Burley Griffin was so fascinated by the native trees and plants that he put this place in his original plan.

The only part of the capital designed with pedestrians in mind is the area around the **Civic Centre.** The original business and shopping district opened in 1927 — by Canberra standards that's ancient history — and is complete with symmetrical white colonnaded buildings in a mock-Spanish style. Nearby are modern shopping malls, the **Canberra Theatre Centre,** and a historic merry-go-round.

One of Canberra's best known landmarks is "Questacon," or the **National Science and Technology Centre.** This hands-on science museum is open daily from 10am–5pm. Entry costs A$8 for adults. Architecturally, it's an interesting study in curves. The low-slung copper-plated dome rests on graceful arches standing in a circular moat. Some say it looks like a flying saucer at rest.

A more conventionally-styled dome covers the vast **Australian War Memorial,** which is a sandstone shrine climaxing a ceremonial avenue called **Anzac Parade.** There are war memorials all over Australia, but this is the definitive one. It's hard to avoid being swept up in the mood of the place as you walk past walls inscribed with the names of more than 100,000 Australian war dead. But beyond the heroic statues and mosaic murals, the memorial is the most visited museum in Australia, with displays of uniforms through the years, battle maps, and plenty of hardware, from rifles to a real World War II Lancaster bomber.

Closer to the lake, one final military monument: the **Australian-American Memorial,** a slim aluminum shaft supporting a stylized eagle with its wings upheld in V-for-victory fashion. It was paid for by public contributions in order to acknowledge US participation in the defense of Australia during World War II.

South of the Lake

 The mostly windowless walls of the **Australian National Gallery** were designed to enclose "a museum of international significance," as official policy decreed. The enterprise has succeeded on several levels, showing off artists as varied as Monet and Matisse, Pollack and de Kooning, and an honor roll of Australian masters. Another indication of the range of interests are the displays of art from Pacific island peoples, black Africa, and pre-Columbian America. One of the high points is the collection of Australian Aboriginal art in the Art of Aboriginal Australia and Torres Strait Islands gallery: dreamily intricate human and animal forms on bark, evolving into the modern version in polymer paint on chipboard, dots and whorls and crosshatching looking at first glance like arbitrary abstractions. The gallery also has a glistening sculpture garden overlooking Lake Burley Griffin.

The **High Court of Australia,** linked to the National Gallery by a footbridge, is a bold, boxy building with an immense expanse of glass on its façade and a stylized waterfall. This last stop for legal appeals bears no resemblance to the Victorian halls of justice elsewhere in the country. But the building is no less impressive for its unconventional looks. Its gigantic public hall is sometimes used for exhibitions and concerts.

Also on the lakefront, the **National Library** houses more than 2 million books. This institution serves scholars and other libraries, and mounts exhibitions of rare books. Its reading room houses an extensive selection of overseas newspapers and magazine publications. There are guided tours, a bookshop, and a pleasant café, the Brindabella Bistro.

Embassy Row, the diplomatic quarter branching out well beyond the leafy suburb of Yarralumla, is a showcase of architectural vanities and charms, well worth a tour by car or sightseeing bus. In the early days of Canberra, diplomats dreaded the prospect of being transferred out to the wilds, and most countries dragged their feet about moving to the new capital until Prime Minister Menzies got tough in the 1950s. The United States was the first nation to open a legation here. Today's US Embassy, set on a hill, is a fine replica of an 18th-century American mansion. Many other nations also decided to erect buildings typical of their cultures, including the Thai embassy with its traditional sweeping roofs and the Indonesian compound adorned with statues of legendary figures. The Japanese embassy has a tea house in its formal garden.

Canberra's Neo-Classical **Old Parliament House** became the seat of government in 1927 and fulfilled that role until being replaced in 1988. It is now the home of the **National Portrait Gallery** and can be visited daily, 9am–4pm. Outside it is the **Aboriginal Tent Embassy,** erected to protest that Aboriginal land rights have not been achieved.

A new, permanent parliament house to replace the old one was dedicated by Queen Elizabeth II in the bicentennial year, 1988. **New Parliament House** can be visited 9am–5pm and there are free guided tours. The interior represents the best in Australian art and design. The Great Hall is dominated by a 20-m (66-ft)- high tapestry. The combination of an unusual design as well as exploding building costs made the new complex, on the site originally selected by Burley Griffin, a surefire cause célèbre during its construction. Taxpayers noted the lavish offices, bars, swimming pool and sauna.

Meanwhile, they're minting it in the southwestern district called Deakin, and you can watch. **The Royal Australian Mint** has a visitors' gallery overlooking the production line where the country's coins are punched out. The factory also "moonlights" to produce the coins of several other countries. The Mint's own museum contains coins and medals of special value.

Other Canberra attractions include the **National Film and Sound Archive** and the **Australian Institute of Sport.** The latter is particularly worth visiting for its interactive sports exhibition called Sportex.

Out of Town

Animal lovers don't have far to go to meet kangaroos, echidnas, wombats, and whatnot. The **National Aquarium and Australian Wildlife Sanctuary** is only a few miles southeast of the city center, in Red Hill. You can walk through acrylic tunnels while sharks cruise past. The bird population includes parrots, kookaburras (the largest kingfishers), cockatoos, and flightless emus.

The **Tidbinbilla Nature Reserve,** situated 40 km (25 miles) southwest of Canberra, is a much bigger affair — thousands of acres of bushland where the native flora and fauna, including kangaroos, wallabies, and koalas, flourish.

Next to this unspoiled wilderness, the **Tidbinbilla Deep Space Tracking Station,** one of only three deep-space tracking stations in the world, takes advantage of its isolation, training its giant antenna on the most intriguing novelties of the cosmos. Australia operates the station in conjunction with the US space agency, NASA. Tidbinbilla is open to the public daily, and has several exhibitions on space exploration.

A.C.T.'s Outpost

Thanks to a bit of historical gerrymandering, landlocked Canberra has a toehold on the South Pacific.

Jervis Bay, a peninsula located on the New South Wales coast, was annexed to the Australian Capital Territory early in the 20th century on the off chance that the future Canberra might need a seaport. It didn't, however. The coastal enclave today includes an uncommon combination of facilities: Inviting dunes and beaches rub shoulders with the Royal Australian Naval College, a missile range, and a National Park. Jervis, named after an English admiral, is correctly pronounced "Jarvis," although locals are starting to rhyme it with nervous. The sand on Jervis Bay beaches is dazzling white. Dolphin cruises operate from the town of **Huskisson** — you almost always get to see dolphins, and sometimes you see migratory whales as well. Not far away, a delightful glade called **Greenpatch** offers some remarkably tame wildlife and multicolored birds.

One of the bay's unusual sights is the wreck of the **Cape St. George Lighthouse.** The placement of this 19th-century beacon was unfortunate. It was built in the wrong place, virtually invisible to northbound ships. Even worse, the construction itself was considered to be a hazard to navigation. To remedy the situation, the navy took aim and reduced it to an historic ruin.

QUEENSLAND

Queensland provides just about everything that makes Australia so desirable, plus some spectacular exclusives of its own. At twice the size of Texas, sunsoaked Queensland gives you the choice of flashy tourist resorts, Outback mining towns, or a modern metropolis; rainfor-

Emus strut through the Tidbinbilla Nature Reserve, near Canberra.

est, desert, or apple orchard. But the most amazing attraction of all is Queensland's offshore wonderland— the longest coral reef in the world, the Great Barrier Reef.

Brisbane's "Old Windmill" (1829): convict-built and treadmill-powered.

Queensland is one of those typical Australian success stories. It was founded in 1824 as a colony for incorrigible convicts, the "worst kind of felons," for whom not even the rigors of New South Wales were a sufficient deterrent. In an effort to quarantine criminality, free settlers were banned from an 81-km (50-mile) radius. But adventurers, missionaries, and hopeful immigrants couldn't be held back for long. Queensland's pastureland attracted many eager squatters, and in 1867 the state joined the great Australian gold rush with a find of its own. Prosperity for all seemed to be just around the corner.

Mining still contributes generously to Queensland's economy. Above ground, the land is kind to cattle and sheep, and warm-hearted crops like sugar, cotton, pineapples, and bananas. But tourism is poised to become the biggest money-spinner, for Queensland is Australia's vacation state.

For touristic purposes the state can be divided into a dozen or more zones, from wild tropical adventurelands in the far north to the sophistication of the Gold Coast in the south. The busiest gateways to all of this are the state capital, Brisbane, and the port of Cairns, which has become one of Australia's most popular tourist destinations.

Brisbane

As befits a subtropical city with palm trees and backyard swimming pools, Brisbane's pace is so relaxed you'd hardly imagine its population was more than a million. The skyscrapers, some quite audacious, have gone a long way towards overcoming the "country-town" image, but enough of the old, elegant, low-slung buildings remain as a reminder of former days; some are wonderful filigreed Victorian monuments, some done up in bright, defiant colors.

In 1859, when Brisbane's population was all of 7,000, it became the capital of the newly proclaimed state of Queensland. The state treasury contained only 7½ pence, and within a couple of days even that was stolen. Old habits of the former penal colony seemed to die hard.

The shy and cuddly koala "bear," a marsupial, is one of the best known examples of Australia's distinctive fauna.

The capital's location, at a bend in the Brisbane River, has made possible some memorable floods over the years, but it sets an attractive stage for Australia's third-largest city. Spanned by a network of bridges (the first dated 1930), the river continues through the suburbs to the beaches and islands of Moreton Bay. Some of Australia's most celebrated types of seafood come from here, notably the gargantuan local mud crabs and the Moreton Bay bug. In spite of its name, this bug, which is related to the lobster, is a gourmet's joy.

Up the hill, on Wickham Terrace, stands an unusual historic building, the **Old Windmill,** also known as the Old Observatory, built by convicts in 1829. Design problems foiled the windmill idea; to grind the colony's grain, the energy of the wind had to be replaced by a convict-powered treadmill. Later, the tower found less strenuous uses as a fire lookout station and a transmitter for early television experiments.

King George Square, next to City Hall, and the nearby **Anzac Square** are typical of the green open spaces that make the center of town breathable. Pedestrians-only is the rule in Brisbane's central Queen Street Mall, flanked by big stores and interspersed with shady refuges and outdoor cafés. This is a place for people-watching. Here, on a fine day, visitors from cooler climes should take a seat to enjoy the warm sun and watch the passersby. The local men go about unselfconsciously in sport shirts and shorts — except for the businessmen, wilting in suits and ties.

Where central Brisbane fits into the bend in the river, the **Botanic Gardens** green the peninsula with countless species of Australian and "exotic" (such as American) trees, plants, and flowers. **Parliament House,** a political hothouse built in the 19th-century Renaissance style, overlooks the gardens and is the headquarters of the state's legislative assembly.

Across the Victoria Bridge from the center of town, the **Queensland Cultural Centre** puts most of Brisbane's cultural eggs in one lavish, modern basket. The south-bank complex includes the **Queensland Art Gallery,** a 2,000-seat concert hall and a comparable theater, and the **Queensland Museum**. The riverside gardens, plazas, restaurants, and cafés round off the scene. There are free guided tours of the art gallery.

If you're looking for a classic Brisbane pub, check out the **Breakfast Creek Hotel** on the north side of a bend in the Brisbane River. It was built in 1889. If you seek bars and restaurants, **Fortitude Valley** is a lively precinct. Brunswick Street, the valley's main thoroughfare, is lined with nightclubs, street cafés, and artsy, sometimes scruffy, little shops. There's an Irish pub and a compact Chinatown. On weekends a market operates. Nightlife there can be fun, but it's wise to take a taxi heading home after dark.

To escape the heat and rush of the city, try **Mount Coot-tha Forest Park,** on the southwest edge of Brisbane. The name is derived from an Aboriginal word meaning "mountain of dark native honey." The spacious park features a giant modern dome enclosing some 200 species of tropical plants. Here, too, you'll find Australia's largest **Planetarium.**

It's only about 11 km (7 miles) to **Lone Pine Sanctuary,** which is home to one of the country's best-known collections of native animals. (By boat the trip is a few miles longer.) The stars of the show are the koalas, mostly sleeping like babies, clinging to their eucalyptus branches. The sanctuary has kangaroos galore. This is also a golden opportunity to get a close-up look at Tasmanian devils, which are red-eared, mousy-looking marsupials the size of a small pig and, unlike the koalas, difficult to love.

Recent developments for visitors include a self-guided tour along the **Albert Street Literary Trail** (a series of 32 bronze plaques bearing quotes about Brisbane) and St. Helena by Night. The latter attraction involves participants boarding a vessel (ominously called the *Cat o' Nine Tails*) at dusk, donning prisoners' garb and setting out from Manly on Morton Bay for **St. Helena Island,** Queensland's former prison.

On **North Stradbroke Island** in Brisbane's Morton Bay, the island's Aboriginal community has developed a 90-minute tour called the **Goompi Trail**. An Aboriginal guide explains the island's flora and fauna, with Dreamtime stories, bush tucker (food), and medicine.

Gold Coast

South of Brisbane, a day-trip distance if you're rushed, the Gold Coast is a Down Under impression of Miami Beach. Although it may be overexploited, it's so dynamic and there are so many opportunities for things to do that you can hardly fault it. And the beach —anything from 30 to 50 km (19 to 31 miles) of it, depending on who's doing the measuring — is a winner in any league. More than 20 Gold Coast surfing beaches patroled by surf lifesavers form the

Blue skies frame the tops of bold skyscrapers in Brisbane, where the climate is ideal.

Typical Gold Coast fun in the sun: aerial view of bathers at the beach.

backdrop for activities ranging from swimming, sailing, and boating to surfboarding and windsurfing.

The trip down the Pacific Highway south from Brisbane (78 km or 49 miles and about an hour's drive) is a study in Australian escapism. In the midst of forest and brushland grows a seemingly inexhaustible supply of amusement parks, luring transient fun-seekers with attractions for all the family: These diverting parks — there are seven major ones — have names like Dreamworld, Sea World, and Wet 'n' Wild.

Warner Bros Movie World, one of the biggest, offers a Hollywood-style experience, including stunt shows, special effects, and large-format amusement rides.

Sea World (foreground), one of the Gold Coast's theme parks, lies just north of Surfer's Paradise.

The **Dreamworld** park operates an attraction claimed to be "the fastest, tallest ride in the world," the Tower of Terror. Visitors thrill to action-packed rides with names like Wipeout and Thunderbolt, watch adventure films on a six-story-high screen or (if they want something quieter) cuddle a koala.

Other Gold Coast theme attractions include **Sea World,** noted for its dolphin displays, and **Wet 'n' Wild,** which contains a giant wave pool, a 45-degree toboggan water drop, and a seven-story speed slide. Nature-lovers can also enjoy **Currumbin Sanctuary,** where masses of squawking rainbow lorikeets are fed each morning and evening. Currumbin is down towards the southern edge of the Gold Coast, which ends at **Point Danger** (so named by Captain Cook when he passed by in 1770). Beyond lies New South Wales.

The essence of the Gold Coast is Surfer's Paradise, as lively as any seaside resort in the world and much addicted to high-rise living. When you're not sunbathing, swimming, or surfing, you can go bungy jumping next to Sea World or just window-shop, eat out, socialize, or wander through the malls, one of which, **Raptis Plaza,** is adorned by a full-scale replica of Michelangelo's David. The pace is hectic, and the revelry goes on as late as you can last. To unwind, take a leisurely boat cruise along the Southport Broadwater or canals of Surfer's Paradise.

A new Surfer's Paradise landmark, not far from Sea World, is **Palazzo Versace,** world's first Versace Hotel, billed as "six star" and filled with Versace trappings.

Surfer's Paradise is approached through a thicket of gas stations, fast-food outlets, and motels — a reconstruction of the outskirts of many an American city, and in similar taste. The conglomeration is skyscrapered in a peculiar way: tall, slim apartment blocks interspersed with bungalows. The tanned, relaxed "beautiful people" you see on the beach today were probably pale, tense yokels a couple of days ago; the irresistible sun does wonders.

The lush green backdrop to the Gold Coast is known as the Hinterland. It encompasses subtropical rainforests, waterfalls and bushwalking tracks, mountain villages and guest houses, craft galleries and farm-stay accommodations.

Sunshine Coast

For the beachy perfection of the Gold Coast with less commercialism (although they're working on it), try the resorts of the Sunshine Coast, north of Brisbane. Some of Australia's best surfing is hiding here.

Inland, the territory is laden with vast plantations of sugar cane, bananas, pineapples, and passion fruit. The area is also a center of production of the prized macadamia nut, named after a 19th-century Australian scientist, John Macadam. Hawaii got into the macadamia growing business later.

The Sunshine Coast resort closest to Brisbane, **Caloundra,** has a beach for every tide. The northernmost town on the Sunshine Coast, **Noosa,** used to be a little-known hideaway of fishermen, surfers, and beachcombers. That was in the 1960s, before the trendsetters from Sydney and Melbourne arrived. But it's still pretty laid back. **Noosa National Park,** a sanctuary of rainforest and underpopulated beaches, occupies the dramatic headland that protects Laguna Bay from the sometimes squally South Pacific breezes. Fraser Island (see page 83) is easily reached from here.

Near **Nambour,** the principal town inland from the Sunshine Coast, you can hardly miss a terribly Australian sort of tourist

Between Queensland's coast and the Reef, emerald islands dot the sea, offering a range of resorts.

Blazing Flowers

Every springtime, as early as August, the roadsides and fields of Western Australia break out in color as the wild flowers bloom. Even the deserts are transformed into flower gardens for the occasion. Many thousands of different species spring up overnight. The big show continues until about October, in all the shades of the spectrum.

Because of Western Australia's isolation, most of the flowering plants are found nowhere else. Flower lovers from all over the continent and abroad flock to see exhibits as vivid as the green and red kangaroo paw, the official floral emblem of the state.

Among the best places to enjoy spectacular displays are Yanchep National Park and the jarrah forests of the south-west. Or you can stay in Perth and see the blooming miracle in miniature in King's Park.

attraction: the monstrously magnified symbol. A startling example is an immense fiberglass replica of a pineapple, as tall as a house — the come-on for a whole tourist complex. A competitor in this field of the ridiculous is The Big Cow, so colossal that you are invited to climb inside. Collectors of kitsch can find additional excesses in the area.

Great Barrier Reef

Australia's biggest and most wonderful sight lies just below the ocean waves. Many millions of minuscule cells multiply relentlessly in fantastic shapes, growing into an infinite variety of forms — and colors from lettuce green to flaming crimson — to create the world's largest living phenomenon. The reef is home to 400 different types of coral. It stretches as far as you can see and beyond:

more than 2,000 km (1,240 miles) of submerged tropical gardens. In among them, the sea is sprinkled with hundreds of paradise islands. About half the size of Texas, the giant reef was proclaimed a marine park by the Australian Government in 1975. The Great Barrier Reef was placed on the World Heritage list in 1981, becoming the biggest World Heritage area in existence. It is now managed by the Great Barrier Reef Marine Park Authority.

Seen more intimately through a diver's mask, the reef is the spectacle of a lifetime, like being inside a boundless tropical fishbowl among the most lurid specimens ever conceived. The fanciful shapes of the coral, gently waving in the tide, might almost lull you to sleep. But not for long. A blazing blue and red fish darts into sight, pursuing a cloud of a thousand minnows. A sea urchin stalks past on its needles; a giant clam opens its hairy mouth as if sighing with nostalgia for its youth, a century ago.

In 1770 Captain Cook was exploring the Australian coast and stumbled upon the Great Barrier Reef: The *Endeavour* was gored by an unsuspected outcrop of coral. Patching the holes as best they could, the crew managed to sail across the barrier, and the vessel limped onto the beach at what is now Cooktown, where some major repairs had to be improvised.

There are many ways of appreciating the coral and its fishy visitors. You can stay dry in a glass-bottom boat, or join a brief cruise aboard a semi-submarine. Or descend into an underwater observatory at the Townsville **Great Barrier Reef Wonderland,** which boasts the world's largest coral reef aquarium. With a mask and snorkel tube you can get close to the underwater world, but the only way to blend totally with the environment is in a weightless state, diving as long and as deep as you please with SCUBA gear. If you're not a qualified diver you can take a crash course at many of the resorts. Organized excursions for advanced divers are also available. In some places the coral stands exposed, but visitors are asked not to walk over it, as that severely damages the living organisms.

The Resort Islands

The reef—actually a formation of thousands of neighboring clumps of reefs—runs close to shore in the north of Queensland but slants ever farther out to sea as it extends southwards. Hundreds of islands are scattered across the protected waters between the coral barrier and the mainland. More than a dozen have been developed into resorts, ranging from spartan to sybaritic. But only two resort islands — Heron and Green — are on the reef itself. From all the others you have to travel, by sea or air, from 5 to 70 km (3 to 43 miles) to reach the main attraction.

Here are some details about the character and facilities of the resorts of the Great Barrier Reef, heading from south to north:

Fraser Island is actually south of the Great Barrier Reef but it is close enough to it, and interesting enough, to rate inclusion in this list. About 120 km (75 miles) long, Fraser is considered to be the largest sand island in the world. But there's more than sand: lakes, marsh, pine forest, and rainforest. This is an island for fishing and beachcombing, not swimming or coral dives. Excursions to the island are available from Noosa (see page 80).

Lady Elliot Island is a coral isle, part of the reef, but situated south of the Tropic of Capricorn. Activities center on diving, swimming, and windsurfing. The gateway airport is in Bundaberg, a sugar-producing town 375 km (232½ miles) up the coast from Brisbane.

Heron Island is heaven for divers. It's a small coral island right on the Great Barrier Reef. Amazing coral and hundreds of species of fish are waiting to be sighted just outside your door. Alternatively, nature lovers can concentrate on the giant green turtles, which waddle ashore between mid-October and March to bury their eggs in the sand. Heron Island is also the goal of thousands of migrating noddy terns and shearwaters. A resort on the island accommodates up to 250 people. There are no day trips and no camping.

Great Keppel Island is one of the larger resort islands in area and in vacation population. The great white beaches are simply gorgeous. The Great Barrier Reef is fully 70 km (43½ miles) away, but Great Keppel is surrounded by good local coral, and there's an underwater observatory. Its beaches are among the best in the resort islands. Great Keppel is also one of the cheapest islands to reach from the mainland — a round-trip ferry trip from Rosslyn Bay costs about A$30. For other angles on the sea's secrets in the area, rent a sailboard, catamaran, motorboat, and/or snorkeling gear from The Beach Shed on Putney Beach. You can also go water-skiing or parasailing.

Brampton Island, an informal resort, is easily reached by air or sea from Mackay. With forested mountains and abundant wildlife, it's worth exploring the mountainous interior of the island. You can also discover neighboring Carlisle Island, uninhabited and connected to Brampton by a reef which is wadeable when the tide's out. If the many sandy beaches don't suffice, there's a saltwater swimming pool.

Lindeman Island, the most southerly of the islands in the Whitsunday archipelago, was named by Captain Cook after the feast of Pentecost, which is approximately the time of year when he passed through. Lindeman Island was almost overrun by feral goats, but they have been eradicated. If you want an all-inclusive vacation you can stay at the Club Med Resort there. There's a campsite as well. You can travel there by boat or fly in with Island Air Taxis from Whitsunday Airport on the mainland.

Hamilton Island. With its jet airstrip, 14-story apartment tower, seven restaurants, 10 bars, a 200-boat marina, and the largest freshwater pool in the Pacific, Hamilton is the slickest international resort in the Coral Sea. It's all carefully thought out, from the busy yacht marina and shops to the landscaping around the Polynesian-style cottages. Divers can rush out to the reef by catamaran or by helicopter. The island's rainbow lorikeets not only eat out of your hand but sit on your arm while doing it. There are tame kangaroos, too.

Long Island is 11 km (7 miles) long — narrow and hilly. Close to the mainland and far from the reef, it has three resorts: Club Crocodile, Long Island Palm Beach Hideaway, and Whitsunday Wilderness Lodge. There's also a campground. Most of the island is national park rainforest.

South Molle Island also consists mainly of national park, plus a resort. South Molle is virtually joined to North Molle Island 2 km away, and to the closer Mid Molle Island. The beaches are good (there are some quiet ones at the south end), and you'll find interesting paths for walks through the hilly bush. Though the Great Barrier Reef is some 60 km (37 miles) away, coral reefs exist nearby.

Daydream Island. The tiniest of all the Barrier Reef resort islands, Daydream snoozes just offshore from busy Shute Harbour. Since beaches are not the island's strongest selling point, Daydream Island International Resort has built swimming pools. The resort accommodates 300 guests. A day trip to the island from Shute Harbour costs about A$25.

Hayman Island, the most northerly of the Whitsunday group, boasts the chic, international-class Hayman Island Resort, a lavish, five-star hotel. Hayman has a marina for drop-in yachts, and a choice of restaurants, bars, and shops. The long, sandy beach suggests all sorts of water-sports, dutifully catered to by the resort's activities staff. Some tiny, uninhabited isles are so close you can walk out to them at low tide.

Magnetic Island is virtually a suburb of Townsville, the biggest city in northern Queensland. Many of the island's 2,500 or so permanent residents commute to work on the mainland by ferry. Being so easy to reach, it's a busy day-trip destination — by sea or helicopter — but Magnetic Island also has plenty of accommodations of all classes. Most of the island is a national park, busy with birds and animals (there are even koalas in the gum trees), and the choice of beaches is enticing. Magnetic Island, "Maggie" to the locals, was given its name by the omnipresent Captain Cook, whose compass broke down here.

Orpheus Island. Famous visitors to Orpheus Island have included Zane Grey and Vivien Leigh half a century ago. Over 100 species of fish and 340 of the 350 known species of Reef coral adorn underwater gardens in the island's several sheltered bays, with the channel at the southern point of Orpheus believed to host the Reef's largest range of soft corals.

Orpheus Island Resort, longest-established resort on the Great Barrier Reef, is one of the few remaining privately owned Australian island resorts.

Nestled in a sheltered bay on the western (mainland) side of the island, the resort accommodates only a maximum of 74 guests in 31 private rooms. Day-trippers and children under 15 are banned.

Hinchinbrook Island basks in a superlative of its own: "The world's largest island national park." A continental rather than coral island, but only 5 km (3 miles) from the reef, Hinchinbrook has a couple of campsites (park rangers issue permits on the mainland) and a small resort with 65 accommodations. Inland from the smooth sand beaches you will find mountains well worth climbing, as well as rainforest, waterfalls, and bushland, where you'll come across wallabies.

Bedarra Island, in the Family Islands group, reachable via neighboring Dunk Island, has a very small, exclusive, and expensive resort on its west coast. It costs over A$1000 a day to stay there, all inclusive. The nearest mainland town is Tully, noted for its annual rainfall average, the highest in the country. Statistically, Tully is twice as wet as Darwin.

Dunk Island is mostly a national park. But one of the best developed resorts fits inoffensively into a corner of the island originally occupied by a World War II radar station. Dunk's genuine tropical rainforest offers a taste of the eternal: vines struggling to grab the sunlight at the expense of the trees they strangle on the way up. All is silence except for a waterfall, the trickle of raindrops off glistening leaves, the fluttering wings of a brightly plumed bird. In the interior you can visit the carefully tended grave of Edmund Banfield, the island's first white resident. A journalist from Townsville, Banfield went to the island in 1898 to die quietly, having been given only weeks to live. He survived for 25 more years, writing books with titles like *The Confessions of a Beachcomber* and *My Tropic Isle*.

Fitzroy Island came into the resort business later than most. It's the object of day excursions from Cairns. Accommodations here are quite limited, but a dining room and regular evening entertainment keep the overnight population well amused. Fitzroy Island's interior is rainforest; the beaches meet anyone's standards, however high. Nudey Beach is one of the best.

Green Island, one of the two resorts actually on the reef, is, like Fitzroy, popular with day-trippers from Cairns, but when the crowds depart, the vacationers occupying the five-star Green Island Reef Resort have the tiny island, and its throngs of seabirds, to themselves. The resort takes 92 guests. Green Island's Underwater Observatory, claiming to be the first of its kind in the world, lets you view the coral garden from a dry vantage point three fathoms below water level. In this situation, the fish come to look through the glass at human beings in the tank. Another attraction, a short walk inland, is Marineland Melanesia, with crocodiles, stingrays, giant turtles, and Melanesian artifacts.

Lizard Island. Situated about 30 km (18½ miles) off the tropical northern coast of Queensland, Lizard has all the trappings of a fictional escape island: with rainforest, mangrove swamps, and a couple of dozen delectable beaches. The island is almost on the edge of one of Australia's most productive game-fishing zones, in which the half-ton black marlin are found. It's favored by millionaires and celebrities, who stay at the exclusive and pricey Lizard Island Resort. The only other alternative is a very basic campground.

Tropical Coast

The coast of mainland Queensland paralleling the Barrier Reef terminates in the north with Cape York Peninsula, one of Australia's wildest and least populated areas. If heading for Cape York, it's best to go with an experienced operator — roads are often little more than dirt tracks. Here are a few highlights further south, from south to north, heading along the Capricorn Coast relentlessly towards the Equator.

Rockhampton sits only a few kilometers north of the Tropic of Capricorn — 23°27' south of the Equator, and the line that officially divides the tropics from the subtropics. From here on northwards, you need no excuse to order an icy beer to assuage your tropical thirst. Rockhampton, known as the beef capital of Australia, has some genuinely interesting Victorian architecture, worth a walking tour. To the north, the Berserker Range offers spectacular limestone caves.

Mackay is the next substantial town, and even by Australian standards it's a long haul — about 340 km (211 miles) — over Highway 1, a road which is not particularly noted for its scenery.

Surrounded by dense green fields of cane, Mackay processes one-third of the nation's sugar crop. At the harbor stands the world's biggest bulk sugar terminal. From July to December you can see cane crushing in progress at the **Farleigh Sugar Mill,** 12 km northwest of the town on the Bruce Highway. The largest national park in Queensland, **Eungella National Park,** lies inland from Mackay, in rugged mountain country. This is one of the few places in Australia where you can see platypuses in the wild. The best time is morning and late afternoon. There's a platypus viewing platform near the bridge in Eungella township.

Proserpine, another sugar town, is inland from Airlie Beach and Shute Harbor, resorts from which there are boat trips to the Whitsunday Islands.

Another 265 km (165 miles) closer to the Equator, and you reach the metropolis of Queensland's far north, **Townsville** (population about 128,000), named after one Robert Towns, a Sydneysider. Townsville is the headquarters of the mining and cattle industries of Queensland's interior and one of the gateways for islands of the Reef. The historic center of town, along the river, contains some photogenic old buildings with filigreed iron balconies or stately columns and arches. Townsville's top attraction is the **Great**

Rainforest of Mossman Gorge, near Cairns in Australia's tropical northwest Queensland.

Barrier Reef Wonderland, with a superb simulation of the reef and a fantastic, colossal aquarium. It's open daily, 9:30am to 5pm.

The landscape changes from dry to lush as you head north to **Cairns,** Townsville's regional rival. Cairns (population about 114,000) is likely within a few years to replace Townsville as Australia's largest tropical city. A port laid out in grid style with huge blocks and extra-wide streets, Cairns has benefited economically from Australia's tourist boom and grown dramatically, but in the process has lost much of its former sleepy, tropical outpost atmosphere. It's an ideal base for regional exploration, within reach of the Great Barrier Reef, the World Heritage-listed Daintree rainforest, the temperate Atherton Tableland, the Outback, and even Cape York Peninsula.

Some 600 tour options are available in Cairns every day and the city has become Australia's foremost center for adventure tourism. No fewer than three hot-air balloon companies operate locally, plus skydiving and numerous whitewater rafting operations.

Diversions in Cairns itself include the **Pier Marketplace** (a shopping and leisure complex), the **Reef Hotel Casino** (four separate gaming areas and a five-star hotel), and **Undersea World Oceanarium** (providing visitors with an introduction to the Great Barrier Reef.) A newcomer (completed in 2000) is **Cairns Central,** the region's largest shopping complex, on the corner of McLeod and Spence Streets. It boasts 180 specialty stores on three levels, a food court, and an entertainment center with six cinemas.

Cairns action begins early in the morning, when speedy catamarans leave for Green Island and Fitzroy Island and smaller boats set sail with scuba divers or fishermen aboard. Big-game fishing is big business in Cairns, where sportsmen hunt black marlin.

Some travel agencies open their doors at 7:30am and keep going until after dark. They sell a large collection of excursions — to Green Island, inland to Kuranda and the Atherton Tableland, and up the coast as far as Port Douglas.

The charming little tourist town of **Kuranda,** "the village in the rainforest," with its craft shops, galleries, and restaurants, is located a short distance northwest of Cairns. Kuranda is linked to Cairns by the wonderfully quaint and picturesque **Kuranda Scenic Railway,** while the **Skyrail Rainforest Cableway** transports guests to Kuranda in six-person aerial gondolas over dense, tangled World Heritage-listed rainforest. You can buy tickets for a round trip — train one way and

Skyrail the other. Skyrail riders can enter the forest on boardwalks at two stations on the way up and view trees from there. A rainforest information and research center is located at Barron Falls Station. The Skyrail experience is even better when it's misty or raining and the gondolas fill with a woody aroma as mists rise from below. Sweeping views of sugarcane plantations, the Coral Sea, beaches, and offshore islands give way to eucalyptus forest and later to the massive fig trees, kauri pines, and twisted vines of the 120-million-year-old rainforest.

The **Tjapukai Aboriginal Cultural Park** at the base of Skyrail is home to the world-renowned **Tjapukai Aboriginal Dance Theatre.** Performances are primal and electrifying. The **Australian**

The Skyway Rainforest Cableway carries you over the lush canopy to Kuranda, "the village in the rainforest."

Darwin, capital of the Northern Territory, lies dramatically on a peninsula in the Timor Sea.

Woolshed has opened in the same complex, offering an experience of life on an Australian farm.

Spectacularly beautiful coastal scenery is the reward along the highway north from Cairns to **Port Douglas.** When the tide is out, Port Douglas's Four Mile Beach is a wide, hard-packed, almost flat sweep of sand suitable for bike races, jogging, or an afternoon or two of simple sunbathing. Just watch out for crocodiles. Once a little fishing village, Port Douglas has hit the tourism trail, but it's more relaxed than Cairns. The fancy **Mirage Resort** is the

flashiest hotel in town. Near it, Quicksilver runs catamaran services to the islands.

For practical purposes, the nearby sugar-milling town of **Mossman** is for many the end of the line. From here northwards it's several hundred hot kilometers to the likeable river port of **Cooktown,** where Captain Cook's battered *Endeavour* was beached in 1770. The James Cook Memorial Museum tells all about it.

The tip of **Cape York Peninsula,** north of Cooktown, is a vast expanse of marshy terrain, prone to flooding and rife with crocodiles,

Aborigines demonstrate their intricate rituals in the Tjapukai Aboriginal Cultural Park, Cairns.

best negotiated in well-equipped four-wheel-drive vehicles. The rivers are impassable from December to March; **Coen** is the last place for supplies and fuel.

NORTHERN TERRITORY

On the surface, the Northern Territory might seem an unpromising tourist destination. Its deserts, torrid tablelands, and rainforests look immensely uninviting. The region is especially discouraging when it's blazing hot. But the wildlife is enchanting, the scenery is magnificent, and the people, though few and far between, welcome the wandering stranger with Outback hospitality and charm.

The population of the self-governing territory totals only around 193,000. Their median age is 28 years, the youngest of any Australian state or territory. About one in five Territorians is an Aborigine, so cultural insights are part of the agenda for foreign visitors. This is the place to find the grandeur and mystery of the most sacred Aboriginal sites.

The Northern Territory covers about one-sixth of Australia's total area. Perhaps surprisingly, roads in the Territory are generally of high standard and a four-wheel drive vehicle is not necessary unless you specifically want to pursue off-road activities. The climate effectively divides the land into two parts: The north, called "The Top End," is lush and very hot. The rest of the Territory, known as "The Centre," has drastically less rainfall. The Red Centre, with its infinite horizons and parched, rugged beauty, fits the stereotype of "Back of Beyond."

Darwin

Australia's northernmost port, capital of the Northern Territory, is a young, prosperous city radiating the optimism of the reborn, for Darwin has survived far more than its share of catastrophes. At a cost of hundreds of lives, it was bombed scores of times in World War II. Rebuilt after the war, it was once again wiped out by a killer cyclone in 1974. Subsequently planners went back to the drawing board to design a bigger and better city. Darwin's deepwater port is being upgraded at a cost of about A$90 million to enhance the city's role as Australia's gateway to Asia.

The 85,000 Darwinians include more than 50 different ethnic groups, including a large Chinese community. This is reflected in the city's array of Asian and Western eating places, ranging from up-market restaurants to budget-priced food stalls at the **Mindil Beach Sunset Markets,** where seaside eating, shopping, and entertainment combine.

Darwin's daytime temperature averages more than 30°C (86°F) virtually year-round. But while transients wilt, the locals know how to withstand the heat. They dress lightly and casually—even businesspeople wear shorts to work — they use air-conditioning and they down a record amount of frosty beer to stave off dehydration. Although elsewhere in Australia a stubby means a small beer, order a stubby in Darwin and you get a two-liter bottle — almost half a gallon. This gives a clue to the Darwin sense of humor; and the jokes are nearly always a pleasant distraction from the heavy-handed heat. Empty beer cans often wind up as the construction material for a flotilla of fanciful boats which compete in Darwin's annual slapstick regatta.

Local chauvinists will admit that Darwin, about 3,000 km (1,860 miles) from Sydney and Perth, is "a trifle isolated." But that doesn't

Dusk in Kakadu National Park (near Darwin), famous for its Aboriginal rock art and dramatic geology.

deter the eager newcomers arriving from all parts of the country—not least of all for such adventurous activities as bungee jumping, parachuting, and bush walking.

City Sights

Historic buildings are the last thing you'd expect to find in a city wiped out by a modern cyclone. But visitors can tour the restored 19th-century buildings that bring to mind the atmosphere of the pioneering days. Darwin's foundation as a permanent settlement dates back to 1839, relatively modern history even by Australian standards.

Government House, overlooking the harbor, is an elegant example of colonial style (opened in 1883). Although a series of cyclones and the wartime bombs badly damaged the building (known as the Seven Gables), it has been put back together in fine form, and is surrounded by lovely tropical gardens. It replaced an earlier building which was eaten by termites.

Dating from 1885, the single-story stone building known as **Brown's Mart** is now a theater for live plays. The building has a checkered past. Built as a miner's exchange, it was converted for use as a police station and subsequently served the community as a brothel.

Also on an offbeat historical theme, the old **Fannie Bay Gaol** was opened for business in 1883. Closed down in 1952, the jail is now a museum, where you can follow the march of penal progress since those rough-and-ready days. The gruesome gallows were last used in 1952.

Other restored buildings include the **Victoria Hotel,** as Victorian as its name (built in 1894), and the former **Admiralty House.** A surviving portion of the old **Anglican Christ Church Cathedral** has been incorporated into the soaring modern building.

A relatively new tourist venue is the **Wharf Precinct,** housing **Indo-Pacific Marine** (live coral displays) and the **Australian Pearling Exhibition;** pearling has had a long history in the area, and the museum traces the industry from its beginnings.

The New Darwin

For the feel of modern Darwin, drift over to the **Smith Street Mall,** a pedestrians-only shopping area in the heart of the restored city. The shady mall, lined with stores, cafés, and restaurants, is the perfect place for people-watching. All kinds of city and rural "locals" congregate in the mall — there's even a walk-through fountain. If you want to take a photo, be forewarned: The "Australian characters" who turn up here don't normally appreciate the attention.

Darwin's **Museum of Arts and Sciences** at Fannie Bay, about 4 km (2.5 miles) from the city center, includes an art gallery. It's worth a visit for its Aboriginal art section and the exhibition commemorating Darwin's destruction by Cyclone Tracey at Christmastime 1974. It killed more than 50 people.

Another building that looks remarkably ambitious for a town of Darwin's size is the **casino,** a white pyramid of a leisure center surrounding the magnet of gambling. Investors have a choice of traditional games in the sophisticated mold of Monte Carlo or the more folksy Australian style. You can try your hand at two-up, the Australian game that's as simple as tossing two coins. The excitement grabs participant and hangers-on alike.

Lovers of tropical flowers will be delighted by every little garden around town, but the ultimate display occupies the **Botanic Gardens,** 34 hectares (84 acres) of the most fetching, fragrant flowers and plants. In addition to the bougainvillea and frangipani, the orchids are a special source of pride.

Back to the seaside for something completely different: Doctors Gully, at the end of the Esplanade, is the site of a strange audience-participation ritual, the feeding of the fish. At **Aquascene,** tourists wade into the sea at high tide (check the local paper for the time) to hand-feed catfish, mullet, bream, milkfish, and other sizeable denizens of the harbor. Thousands of fish turn up here daily for the festivities, returning to deep-sea pursuits until the next free handout.

Feeding times depend on the tide. Tel. (08) 8981 7837. Entry is $4.50 for adults; bread is free.

Other cities are built around a central business district or a park, but Darwin stretches in all directions around its airport. This is handy for airline passengers but less so for the locals, who must go miles out of their way to get from one part of town to another if the two places happen to be on opposite sides of the runway.

On the north side of the airport near the Casuarina High School is a moving monument to the victims of Cyclone Tracy. It's in the form of a "sculpture" of twisted iron girders, like roller coaster tracks gone wild. No artist produced this abstraction; it's merely the way three girders were contorted when the big wind destroyed a nearby building.

The devastation caused by Cyclone Tracy taught everyone a lesson in architecture and engineering. Now specially reinforced roof construction is required by law; houses should never again go sailing away. Even Darwin's **Chinese Temple,** notwithstanding its sweeping roofs, is guaranteed cyclone-proof. It serves Buddhists, Taoists, and Confucians.

East of Darwin

In the tropical wilderness east of Darwin you can see natural phenomena known as **"magnetic anthills,"** which are found scattered like prehistoric dolmens in the bush alongside the highway. "Magnetic anthills" is a neat expression describing the insect equivalent of skyscrapers. But, to be accurate, they are neither magnetic nor anthills. These termite mounds, often taller than people, are always aligned exactly north-south, for reasons only termites can explain. They look like two-dimensional sandcastles.

Fogg Dam, 60 km (37 miles) east of Darwin, is a splendid sanctuary for a dozen species of water bird coexisting on magical pools. This was the site of the **Humpty Doo** rice project, a multi-million-dollar scheme to grow rice without the disadvantages of the traditional feet-in-the-mud, aching-back method. According to the plan devised by the efficiency experts, airplanes effortlessly seeded the area in one fell swoop. Countless swarms of birds, not having been consulted, feasted on this manna from heaven as soon as the seeds hit the ground. Riceless, Humpty Doo had a great fall and went out of business. The area is again strictly for the birds.

Kakadu National Park

Birdwatchers, botanists, and all other visitors are enthralled by Kakadu National Park, which is situated about 220 km (136 miles) east of Darwin. The scenery ranges from romantic to awesome. As an unparalleled outdoor museum of ancient Aboriginal art, the park is on the World Heritage List of places of "outstanding universal value" deserving protection. Timeless paintings on Kakadu's rock ledges are brimming with mystery and meaning. Some have remained here

"Cathedral"-type termite mounds in tropical Kakadu National Park, two hours drive from Darwin.

since the era of Europe's Paleolithic cave art.

Nineteen different clans of Aboriginal peoples live in the park's 6,144 sq km (2,372 sq miles), between the Wild Man and East Alligator rivers. They lease the land to the National Parks and Wildlife Service and participate in the park's management, including working as park rangers.

Nature has quite bluntly divided Kakadu into two worlds: the plains, with their lagoons and creeks, and the escarpment, a stark sandstone wall marking the western edge of Arnhem Land. From the top of the high plateau waterfalls tumble to the lowlands in the wet season (November to March). The floodplains entertain water birds by the thousand. Their names alone turn laymen into dedicated birdwatchers: white-throated grasswren, white-lined honeyeater, and white-breasted whistler, to list but three of the species that breed in the park. The star of the show, though, is the jabiru, a stately variety of stork.

A Wedge-tailed Eagle at Kakadu National Park, a birdwatcher's paradise.

In the mangroves you'll see striated heron, little kingfisher, and broad-billed flycatcher. And you can go down the checklist with magpie goose, black shag, ibis, and crested plover. A special delight is the sight of the delicately poised lotus bird, which walks miraculously on the water.

The waterways are rich in the eminently edible barramundi. Less appetizingly, the estuaries are home to the saltwater crocodile, which preys on barramundi, birds, small animals, and, on special occasions, human beings.

Kakadu's Rock Art

At as many as a thousand different places in the park, ancient Australians left works of art — rock paintings in styles both primitive and eerily sophisticated.

Ubirr Rock, Kakadu National Park, a World Heritage site.

The earliest legacy consists of arrangements of handprints and the imprints of objects that were dyed and thrown at cliff walls and cave ceilings for decorative effect. Many centuries later, abstract-expressionist artists were to reinvent a similar splashy technique.

The next generation of prehistoric artists concentrated on the figures of animals. Among them is a curious variety of anteater believed to have become extinct perhaps 18,000 years ago, a valuable clue to the age of some of these paintings. The same school of artists painted stick-figure humans in hunting and battle scenes using ochre pigments for color.

Later artists introduced movement into their pictures, such as hunters throwing spears or boomerangs. An innovation of this era was the use of abstract marks around certain figures, like a modern cartoonist's squiggles representing a character's surprise or fear.

A few thousand years after this, Aboriginal artists developed a remarkable style, now called X-ray painting. The profile of, say, a fish is clearly painted but instead of its scales we see its bones and internal organs, with the emphasis on edible or otherwise useful parts.

After Australia was colonized, Europeans, too, became a subject for Aboriginal artists. There are pictures of the sailing ships the British arrived in, and caricatures, scarcely flattering, of the new settlers holding recognizable muskets.

Katherine Gorge

The most spectacular natural attraction located at the Top End of the Northern Territory, Katherine Gorge is about 350 km (217 miles) "down the Track" from Darwin. The Track is what they call the highway linking the Timor Sea and Alice Springs in the **Red Centre of Australia.** Originally a rough path fit for bullock carts and camel trains servicing the overland telegraph line, the route was upgraded by the Americans in World War II to supply Darwin, which was dangerously isolated and under attack.

Katherine, to be precise, is not just a single gorge but a series of 13 gorges. In the wet season (from November to March) the torrents, waterfalls, whirlpools, and rapids give an impression of thundering power. But it's uncomfortably hot and humid, and sometimes the rains cut off the roads. So Katherine Gorge National Park is best visited in the dry season (April to October), when the water flows at a relative trickle. Flat-bottom boats cruise along the river, which reflects sheer cliffsides; walks and hikes offer other perspectives.

Among the sights are Aboriginal wall paintings portraying kangaroos and other native animals, bigger than life-size. Live kangaroos may be seen in the park, as well as the echidna (spiny anteater) and the dingo. Adding a tremor of excitement, there are glimpses of a freshwater variety of crocodile called Johnstone's Crocodile. Unlike the "salties" of the north, though, these fierce-looking reptiles are timid fish-eaters; fortunately, tourists do not figure on their menu. Bird life is colorful, and includes hooded parrots, black cockatoos, and agile rainbow-colored birds.

Alice Springs

Traffic lights have slightly tamed the adventurous Outback atmosphere of Alice Springs, the biggest town for a thousand miles around. "The Alice" still looks rather like the frontier town you imagined: a relaxed, friendly, slightly disheveled community of pioneers, dreamers, transients, and, more recently, throngs of tourists.

The Northern Territory's second biggest population center in the Red Centre has more than 26,000 inhabitants. When it comes to climate, they are extremists. In the summer it gets as hot as 42°C (108°F) but, mercifully, the nights in June, July, September, and October require a sweater or two. Chances of seeing rain are slight. The Henley-on-Todd Regatta, a whimsical fixture each August, is run on the sandy bed of the sometime Todd River, a wide *wadi* gullying through the center of town. The boats, of many classes, are all bottomless, hilariously propelled by the racing legs of their crews.

The Alice first grew around a waterhole discovered in 1871 by the surveying party stringing the first telegraph line from Adelaide to Darwin—and from there to the rest of the world. Alice Springs was named after Alice Todd, who was the wife of South Australia's postmaster general. He won himself a knighthood for pushing through the project; locally, the Todd River immortalizes him.

Camels, traditionally ridden by experts from Afghanistan, brought the equipment for the telegraph relay station built at Alice Springs and the supplies to keep the technicians alive. When the termites devoured the first telegraph poles, replacements — heavy iron poles from in Britain — also had to be transported by camel train.

Telegrams aside, Alice Springs remained isolated until World War II. And until the 1960s it was a crossroads market town. Now it's thriving as a staging post for tourist jaunts throughout the Red Centre.

Like many an Australian town, The Alice is bigger than you might expect, but the essentials can be taken in on a walking tour. In the main street, **Todd Street,** is the **John Flynn Memorial Museum,** dedicated to the founder of the flying doctor service, and **Adelaide House,** the first hospital, which is now a museum. In nearby Parsons Street is the **Old Stuart Town Gaol,** dating from the beginning of the 20th century, complete with "his" and "hers" dormitory cells.

The **Royal Flying Doctor Service,** which brings health care to the farthest cattle ranch, began in Alice Springs in 1928. You can take a tour of the base, on the south side of town. Another service which eased development of the Outback, the **School of the Air,** a radio link with isolated pupils, is headquartered on Head Street.

A couple of kilometers (a little more than a mile) north of town, an unspoiled park surrounds the restored **Telegraph Station.** This was the most important relay station on the line. Before the wires were strung a message could take three months to reach London from Adelaide. The relics here give a glimpse of 19th-century technology and the lonely life of the telegraph pioneers.

South of The Alice on the Ross Highway is a **camel farm,** offering rides atop swaying beasts, the descendants of the camels that supplied the pioneers. It also houses snakes and lizards in the **Arid Australia Reptiles Display.** In July each year, the local Lions Club sponsors the Camel Cup — an exciting day of camel races at Blatherskite Park. The animals are launched from a kneeling start in a cloud of dust, and run just as fast as race horses, though less gracefully.

The **Todd Tavern** at the top of **Todd Mall** is the town's liveliest drinking spot. There's also an "international standard" casino, **Lasseters,** on Barrett Drive. Enthusiasts have a choice of blackjack, roulette, and a sophisticated version of the Australian game of two-up (see page 135), along with the excitement of poker machines and keno, a game resembling bingo.

An eccentric enterprise on Petrick Road southeast of town, desert winery **Chateau Hornsby** produces 1,000 cases of wine a year. Here, in "Australia's farthest winery from anywhere," wines grow in coarse red sand under a fierce sun. They need to be irrigated daily. The resulting wines, with quaint names such as Horny Tawny, may be sampled on the spot.

Alice Springs Desert Park, which has gained worldwide recognition for its achievements in breeding rare and endangered

A 1920s hospital bed looks pristine at Adelaide House.

species, is located about 3 km (1.8 miles) out of town along Larapinta Drive. A visit starts with a 20-minute film, then you tour walk-through enclosures and see the desert animals. It's instructive and entertaining.

A popular excursion from The Alice concentrates on Standley Chasm, 50 km (31 miles) to the west. This passage through the MacDonnell Ranges dwindles to the narrowest gap. The walls are so high and steep that the sun penetrates the bottom only fleetingly at midday. A few slender trees bravely sprout from the rockface high above, reflected in the cool, still water of a natural pool at the far end of the gorge. In the wet season, from November to March, rainwater can suddenly flood the chasm.

The recently paved **Mereenie Loop Road** links Alice Springs with the remote desert points of

An enormous crocodile leaps up from the Adelaide River.

Kings Canyon and **Yulara,** the latter being the site of Uluru (Ayers Rock). The loop forms a dedicated tourism drive called **Pioneer's Path,** which heads through the western MacDonnell Ranges on its way into Alice Springs. The trip covers about 1,200 km (750 miles) and takes

Kings Canyon, one of the dramatic geological attractions on Pioneer's Path in the Northern Territory Outback.

between three and five days, giving an incredible Outback experience on the way.

☛ Uluru (Ayers Rock)

As the sun begins to sink beyond the rim of the desert, the crowds with their cameras gather by car and bus along "Sunset Strip," the tongue-in-cheek name for a dusty stretch of parking lot. As the onlookers watch Ayers Rock undergo its striking changes of color, they are not solemn but rather festive, friendly, and relaxed — in fact, very Australian. By coming here, they are fulfilling an Australian dream, getting to know this mystical, 500-million-year-old rock that rises up from the red heart of the country.

The world's greatest rock, seemingly dropped by divine design in the middle of nowhere, actually protrudes from a buried mountain range. At about 350 m (1,148 ft) high and some 8 km (5 miles) around, it is even more impressive than the dimensions suggest. Standing alone in a landscape as flat as a floor, and tinted as bright as in your imagination, the monolith lives up to its reputation. You'll need no complicated explanations to understand why the Aborigines consider it sacred.

The Aborigines have owned Ayers Rock (known to them as Uluru) under Australian law only since 1985; the small local Aboriginal community leases it back to the government for use as a national park in return for a healthy income as well as participation in its management.

For the Aborigines it's not just a rock, it's a vital aspect of Dreamtime, encompassing the creation of the earth, linked with the life of the present and future. Various parts of the monolith are qualified as sacred sites; they are signposted, fenced off, and barred to outsiders.

The most inspiring views of the rock are to be seen at dawn and dusk. It's well worth getting up at six in the morning to stake out the mighty silhouette from 20 km (12½ miles) away, waiting for the sunrise. As first light strikes the lonely monolith it catches fire, glowing red, then orange, finally seeming to emit rays of wondrous power. Only then the desert world comes to life: a hawk squawks, a rabbit rustles the brush, and hordes of pesky flies begin to buzz. Waving your hand in front of your face soon becomes second nature in the Outback, like a horse flicking its tail. Insect repellent helps, too, but the flies seem to outnumber the people 20 to one. Maybe this is why Aboriginal legends mention bothersome flies.

Sunset offers a most dramatic view of Uluru, an Aboriginal holy site, a world-renowned geological formation.

If you're fit you can join the crowds climbing the rock, although local Anangu Aboriginal people regard this as disrespectful. A few hours suffice for the round-trip via the marked trail, which has a protective chain you can grab when the going gets too steep or windy. The ascent requires no mountain-climbing experience or equipment, but do wear sensible rubber-soled shoes and carry drinking water. From ground level the climbers attaining the summit look like a line of very tired ants. Some climbers die during the experience; they are commemorated by plaques placed discreetly on the base of the rock. The plaques reveal causes of death to be generally heart-attack among older climbers and fatal plunges by younger ones.

Another worthwhile (and safer) way to get to know the rock is to join a walking tour led by a park ranger, circumnavigating the base.

Up close, the monolith discloses its variegated surface, with its caves, dry rivulets, furrows, wounds and gashes, and what might be taken for fanciful engravings 60 m (197 ft) tall. Or take a 20-minute flight from Alice Springs to view the rock and its surroundings from the air.

Only 36 km (22 miles) by road west of Ayers Rock, and visible from its summit, is another stupendous rock formation, **The Olgas.** From afar, **Mount Olga** and its satellites look like a scattering of dinosaur eggs or sleeping elephants, but they're even higher than Ayers Rock. Here, too, dawn and dusk color the most fascinating views, the fantasy shapes changing with the hues and the movement of the shadows. You can get to know the Olgas by a choice of hiking routes. The popular trail from the Katatjuta car park up to the lookout is officially called "suitable for family

The contours of Uluru display many facets, each of which has some symbolic meaning.

enjoyment," but it's steep and tricky enough to deter both the very youngest and oldest generations.

Yulara Development

To cope with hundreds of thousands of visitors each year at Ayers Rock, a comprehensive resort has been built. It could have been a disastrous blot on the landscape, but the Yulara Ayers Rock Resort fits in benignly, 20 km (12½ miles) from the rock. Almost entirely camouflaged, the complex is too low-slung to detract from the majesty of the surroundings.

The facilities start with sites for tents and caravans, and go up to a five-star hotel with gardens, pool, spa, restaurants and bars, television, and in-house video; and of course air-conditioning. It makes for quite a change after a day spent slogging through the desert. The visitors' center in the hotel and shopping complex offers information, literature, and audiovisual shows explaining the desert, the wildlife, geology, mythology, and other angles to enhance your appreciation of the Red Centre.

Several airlines serve Yulara, and the views of the desert on the way are spellbinding. Otherwise you can take a bus or drive; it's about 450 km (279 miles) by paved road from Alice Springs, a whole day to become acquainted with the desert in its many forms — flat and desolate, or covered with scrub, thinly forested, or, more rarely, sand undulating in postcard-worthy dunes.

The best time of year to visit is between May and October, when the days are sunny and warm and the nights refreshingly chill. In January, by contrast, the mean maximum temperature is 36.6°C (98°F), not quite conducive to hiking.

Surviving the Outback

Three-quarters of Australian land is desert — "burning wastes of barren soil and sand," as Henry Lawson described it. These vast empty spaces on the map hold an irresistible challenge for the most intrepid adventurers. Only vaguely comparable with desert of the Sahara type, the far Outback supports vegetation—sometimes even luxuriant—and fascinating wildlife. If you do want to venture off the surfaced roads and explore the unknown, there are a few precautions you must take.

•Do not even consider driving into the Outback in the summer; the heat is unbearable. In the 1840s, explorer Charles Sturt recorded temperatures of 69.5°C (157°F) in the open and 55.5°C (132°F) in the shade. It was hot enough to melt the lead in his pencil and force screws out of wooden boxes. Just think what it could do to your car!

•Rain can also be a source of disaster; after many years of drought, it can suddenly down pour for an entire week, and the land is transformed into an enormous flood plain. So make sure you never camp in a dry riverbed.

Mysterious Kata Tjuta (The Olgas) literally "many heads," are a series of 36 striking dome-shaped peaks.

Frilled-neck lizard, a ubiquitous denizen of the Outback.

•Your vehicle should be a reliable four-wheel-drive, with a complete set of spare parts: two spare tires and tire repair kit, two spare tubes, coil, condenser, fan belt, radiator hoses and distributor points, a tin of radiator leak fixative, spark plugs, an extra jack (with a large baseplate to prevent sinking in sand or mud), 5 liters (quarts) of engine oil, a pump, a tool-kit, an axe, and a small shovel. Keep the gasoline tank full and carry at least 20 liters in reserve.

•You will need reliable maps, and you should plan your route in detail — and stick to the plan relentlessly. At your point of departure, advise the police of your route, the estimated time of arrival at your destination, and the amount of rations you are carrying. Report to the police again when you arrive. Always seek local advice about the hazards you may encounter. If you wish to enter Aboriginal lands, you must first obtain permission from the Aboriginal landowners, and at least four weeks' notice is required. Inquire at the government tourist office for the appropriate address. In some areas you have to be equipped with a two-way radio.

•Take adequate supplies. Most important is water — you will need 6 liters (quarts) per person per day, best carried in metal containers. Emergency rations should be made up of high-energy foods such as dried fruit, with canned meats, soup, and fruit drinks. Some invaluable components of your first-aid kit will be aspirin, water-purifying tablets, salt tablets, diarrhea pills, insect repellent, disinfectant, bandages, and sun-block cream. Your personal survival kit, which should be carried with you at all times, must contain a compass, map, whistle, waterproof matches, pocketknife, bandage, and adhesive plaster.

•Other essentials: a set of billycans (pails or pots with lids and wire bails), several sheets of heavy-duty plastic (2 m (6½ ft) sq), and a length of rubber or plastic tubing. A piece of nylon rope (30 m/98½ ft long) may also be useful.

•Wear loose, light cotton clothing and cover your head. Space blankets can prove a boon: the shiny aluminum side turned towards the sun reflects heat away from the body, keeping the temperature normal. To keep warm, turn the shiny side inwards.

•Do not drive at night. Kangaroos are a real hazard, and you may collide with wild water buffalo, attracted to the roads at night because the surface is warmer than the ground itself.

In Case of Catastrophe

If your car breaks down, above all do not panic. Stay with your vehicle; it will be a welcome source of shade, and it is more easily spotted by aircraft.

•Make visible distress signals, using brightly colored clothing or any available material—anything that contrasts with the earth.

•Move as little as possible, to conserve body fluid. All physical exertion should take place during the cool night hours.

•Your main preoccupation must be water. It is important to ration your supply and set about collecting more by making a solar still, using the following instructions: Dig a hole about 1 m (3 ft) sq and 50 cm (about 20 inches) deep, away from any shade. Place a large billycan (pail or pot) in the bottom of the hole, and surround it with leafy foliage. Cover the hole with a sheet of plastic and seal the edges completely with earth, making sure that the plastic does not touch the interior walls of the hole. If you have a length of rubber or plastic tubing, place it in the bottom of the billycan before you seal the edges of the sheeting, leaving the other end outside to act as a siphon. Place a small stone in the center of the plastic sheet, right over the billycan. Moisture from the ground will condense on the underside of the plastic sheet and will drip slowly into the billycan. In this way you will collect about 2 liters (2 quarts) of water per hole per day, so it's best to make several stills, at least 3 m (about 10 ft) apart. You will need to change the position of the still every three to four days.

•Small animals — frogs, lizards, and snake — are attracted to the stills and may provide an extra source of food. In principle, anything that walks, crawls, swims, flies, or grows from the soil is edible — or so they say. But beware of anything that has a bitter taste and of plants with a milky sap.

•Another source of food and water in the northwest of Australia is the bottle-tree, which preserves water in its hollow trunk for months after the wet season. In an emergency you can also eat the rind of bottle-tree pods, chopped up and stirred with water — nourishing but certainly not gourmet fare.

The prospects may seem harrowing, but after all, the Aboriginals have survived and even thrived in this forbidding land for at least 50,000 years.

WESTERN AUSTRALIA

When it comes to elbow room, the state of Western Australia has no competition. It's a Texas sort of place, though bigger than Texas and Alaska combined, and more than ten times the area of Great Britain.

Most of the state's vast expanse is desert, semi-desert, or otherwise difficult terrain. The bulk of the population of about 1,860,000 has therefore gravitated to the Mediterranean climate found around the beautiful capital city of Perth. Closer to Jakarta than to Sydney, Perth faces the Indian Ocean with an open, outward-looking stance. Here, the cares of the big population centers of eastern Australia seem worlds away.

The state's Outback produces great wealth, and even the forbidding deserts are bursting with minerals. It was gold that brought the state's first bonanza, in the 1880s and 1890s, followed by nickel, bauxite, and iron. Much more appealing are the above-ground riches: the hardwood forests, the orchards, and the vineyards. And, since the climate is so sunny, it's only fair that there is a beach for every possible mood along the 6,400 km (3,968 miles) of coastline.

The first European to set eyes on a Western Australian beach (in 1616) was Dirk Hartog, a Dutch navigator making his way from the Cape of Good Hope to Java. It was not long before other Dutch travelers touched base here, and one of them reported spotting a wallaby, though not by name; he thought it was a giant cat with a pouch for its kitten. Later in the 17th century, the British adventurer William Dampier happened upon Shark Bay, near Carnarvon, and could hardly wait to leave: The land seemed hopeless for farming, there was no drinking water, and he dismissed the natives as "brutes."

More than 200 years after Hartog's discovery of Western Australia, the British finally got around to colonizing it. The site chosen, on the Swan River, became Perth. But what the Colonial Office considered a good idea turned out to be less brilliant in practice. It would take more than the scenery and the climate to attract settlers to what seemed, even by Australian standards, the end of the world. Problems of development persisted, including poor communications, financial difficulties, and a shortage of workers. Prospects for the new frontier became so precarious that the colony's leaders had to make an appeal to London, asking the government to send over a supply of forced laborers — convicts.

Still, nothing really worked in Western Australia until the gold rush toward the end of the 19th century, when the population quadrupled in ten years. Once it was launched on the road to prosperity, there was no stopping the largest state. Its isolation finally ended in the early years of the 20th century when the transcontinental railway linked Perth and Sydney. Western Australia reached new heights of self-confidence and fame in 1983, when the yacht *Australia II* wrested the America's Cup from the US there, for the first time in 132 years.

Perth

Bright new high-rise office buildings scrape the clear blue skies of Perth. If this city brimming with vigor and enthusiasm were a person, you might imagine it had been born with the proverbial silver spoon in its mouth: a handsome, clean-cut youngster with every possible advantage, inevitably growing up to become an unqualified success in life.

Although history refutes the silver-spoon theory, you can't miss Perth's easy self-confidence. The people are relaxed, friendly, and anxious to help the stranger. They are proud of their efficient town and its up-to-date facilities — the stylish shopping arcades, the art galleries, and **Entertainment Centre** — and the great sailing, swimming, surfing, and fishing right on its doorstep. The inhabitants won't fail to inform you that this tidy city sprawling magnificently along the looping river is Australia's sunniest state capital.

Sunshine aside, Perth has called itself "the city of lights" since the early days of the American manned space program. As John Glenn, the first American to orbit the earth, passed over the city, middle-of-the-night Perth switched on every light bulb in town. The friendly gesture brightened the lone astronaut's flight and put Perth's name in lights.

City Sights

Few will get a chance to enjoy a spaceman's perspective, but the view over Perth from **King's Park** is a good compromise for sizing up the city below. These 400 hectares (988 acres) of natural woodland and wild flowers, manicured lawns and picnic sites, solemn monuments and lively playgrounds, are found on the top of a bluff

called **Mount Eliza,** right on the edge of the city center. From here you look down on the wide Swan River as it meanders toward the sea, on the business district with its gleaming skyscrapers, and on the complexity of the well-landscaped municipal freeway system.

The **Swan River** was named after the indigenous black swans found here, first noted with amazement by the 17th-century Dutch navigator Willem de Vlaming. Unlike swans in the Northern Hemisphere, which are white and prone to whistling or grunting when they are not naturally mute, the black swans sound off like a band of clarinets noisily tuning up. They're

Downtown Perth, viewed from King's Park.

The famous black swans of Lake Monger in Perth are as noisy as they are beautiful.

such tame creatures that they'll take bread out of the palm of your hand without biting.

The Swan River begins about 240 km (149 miles) inland in the wheatlands of Western Australia. For most of its long journey, under the name of Avon River, it is only seasonally navigable, and occasionally is downright treacherous. Although here, with the Indian Ocean close enough to salt it, the Swan widens into a lake, and invites reflection — and flotillas of breezy sail boats. By the riverside in the center of town, the **Old Courthouse** really is old, especially by local standards. Built in Georgian style in 1836, it's the oldest public building in Perth.

Stirling Gardens, surrounding the courthouse, is a restful hideaway. The "Ore Obelisk" monument here looks like a giant shishkebab impaling all of the minerals produced in Western

Australia; but don't expect to find gold or diamonds on the skewer — they don't seem to count.

Town Hall, at the corner of Hay and Barrack Streets, was built in the 1860s by convict labor. If you look closely at the outline of the windows of the tower, you may perceive the design of broad arrows — the prison symbol that was stenciled on convict uniforms.

Similarly Tudor in inspiration, but even less of an antique than the Town Hall, **London Court** is a 1930s shopping mall done up in touristy 16th-century style, leaded windows and all. It fits in quite happily with the modern stores and interconnecting shopping precincts radiating from the **Hay Street Mall,** the main shopping street of Perth. Cars are prohibited here, so the window-shopping is very relaxed. The mall is usually animated by buskers — street musicians, magicians, jugglers, or mimes.

A couple of blocks north of here, across **Murray Street Mall,** brings you to **Forrest Place** on the corner of Wellington Street. Here, in Albert Facey House, you'll find the Perth Visitor Center (Tel. 1300 361 351) — an abundant source of brochures, maps, tickets, tours, and bright ideas, all cheerfully dispensed.

In a city as young as Perth, with its skyline of tall, modern office buildings, those historic structures which have escaped the developer's demolition ball are proudly pointed out to visitors.

Government House, found on the main street, St. George's Terrace, is the official residence of the Western Australia governor. Its Gothic effects date from the 1860s. Built by hard-working convicts, the house is used nowadays for a variety of state occasions and as a place to put up visiting VIPs.

The elegant terrace leads directly to the **Barracks Archway,** the last vestige of a headquarters building of the 1860s. This crenellated three-story structure has been preserved as a memorial to the early colonists. Behind the brick archway you can catch a glimpse of the **Parliament House,** where the state legislature holds forth.

You can relax and watch the waves at the Indiana Tea Rooms, Cottesloe Beach, Perth.

On the other side of the railway tracks — you can cross the unusual Horseshoe Bridge by foot or car — stands the **Old Gaol,** built and used by convicts in 1856. Now it's part of the **Western Australia Museum.** The museum offers more than penal relics of the wild-west days. There is also an extensive collection of Aboriginal rock paintings, headdresses, and weapons, and a meteorite that weighs 10 metric tons (11 tons).

The **Western Australia Art Gallery,** close by, shows paintings from several continents.

Also north of the city center is the **Northbridge** district, full of ethnic restaurants, pubs, and nightclubs, especially around James and Lake Streets. If you're in the mood for gambling, go to **Burswood Casino** near the **Causeway Bridge.** Here you'll find more than 140 gaming tables, plus a cabaret, restaurants, and bars, all under one roof.

Back in the center of town: You can hardly miss the Entertainment Centre on Wellington Street. Not quite Perth's answer to the Sydney Opera House, this roundhouse landmark can pack in 8,000 fans for rock groups or ballet. Another cultural focus is the **Concert Hall,** headquarters of the state's symphony orchestra. If you are looking for stage plays, the most atmospheric house is **His Majesty's Theatre,** now restored to its sumptuous Edwardian standard.

Underwater World, an underwater-tunnel aquarium with interactive displays, offers whale-watching trips in season. For action entertainment, experience thrill rides at Adventureworld Theme Park. Nearby, daredevils can try their hand at bungee-jumping from a 12-m (40-ft) tower, or parasail to see the sights of the city from a higher perspective.

The Western Australia Cricket Association (WACA) grounds viewed from the air, Perth.

Beautiful Matilda Bay hugs the city of Perth and is ideal for sailing.

To the Coast

It's only 19 km (12 miles) down the river from Perth to the capital's Indian Ocean port, **Fremantle** — an enjoyable outing on one of the cruise boats that ply the Swan River.

The river tours begin in the center of Perth, at the **Barrack Street Jetty.** On the south side of the **Narrows Bridge,** note the **Old Mill,** built in 1835, an imposing white windmill in the Dutch style from the first half of the 19th century. Perfectly restored, it's open for visits 10am to 4pm.

Beyond this, on the opposite shore, spreads what looks like another transplant from Europe. The campus of the **University of Western Australia** was built and landscaped in a Mediterranean style, from the shrubs right up to the orange-tiled roofs.

Matilda Bay harbors only a relative handful of the swarms of sail boats that call the Swan River home. During World War II this was a base for Catalina flying boats. The bay is the site of the Royal Perth Yacht Club, where the America's Cup was treasured behind bullet-proof glass from 1983 until it was lost to the United States in 1987. New Zealand has since won it, and it's now carefully tucked away in Auckland.

The coastline of the Dalkeith district, near **Point Resolution,** is reasonably enough called Millionaires' Row. The view of these fine mansions from the perspective of the river just might evoke a

With all of the watersports at Cottesloe Beach in Perth, there is never a dull moment for the rescue team.

Lake Cave, one of the spectacular natural wonders of Margaret River.

dash of envy; even millionaires from out of town could become jealous at the sheer opulence of these homes.

Freshwater Bay was named by the crew of *H.M.S. Beagle,* the survey ship made famous as the vehicle for Charles Darwin's researches into natural selection. Beyond this bay, and a zigzag, the river tapers to a fairly narrow-gauge artery spanned by two bridges. Long-suffering convict labor built the first bridge at this site in 1866. It proved a boon to one of its creators, a celebrated outlaw named Moondyne Joe, an escape artist. The night before the ribbon-cutting ceremony, he broke out of Fremantle Prison and gave himself the honor of becoming the first, if unofficial, pedestrian to cross the bridge over the River Swan. He made a clean getaway.

Fremantle

Although it's a serious international port, you'll remember the city of Fremantle for its casual charms. A Mediterranean-style sunniness combines with a Victorian quaintness to give Fremantle its special character. The town may be cosmopolitan, but it is also as down-to-earth as its classic examples of convict architecture.

For years Fremantle — Freo to the Aussies — lay becalmed, a long way from the big time of tourism. Then came the America's Cup saga and a sudden saturation of world attention. New pride inspired the townsfolk in their sparkling campaign to restore the old terraced houses and other relics in time for the 1986/87 defense of the Cup. At the same time, the marina facilities were also vastly expanded and improved.

Whether you think of Fremantle as a yachting base or a workaday port, you'll want to see the sights of the harbor. There is a mixture of dream yachts, trawlers, ocean liners, and cargo ships of every stripe.

Fremantle's highest point is **Monument Hill in War Memorial Park.** There are three memorials altogether, including one for the US personnel based in Fremantle who died in World War II. Another, an original periscope, commemorates the British and Allied submarine crews who perished in the same conflict. This is the place to watch the sun set over the Indian Ocean.

Back near the waterfront, and wasting an enviable view, the 12-sided Round House looks like the forbidding, windowless prison it used to be. Actually it's much more cheerful from the inside, with its sunny courtyard. Built in 1831, the Round House specialized in the lesser criminals, although it was the site of the state's first hanging; generally, incorrigibles were shipped off to the rigors of Tasmania.

The **Western Australian Maritime Museum** was built by convicts to house the Commissariat, the bureaucracy in charge of them.

Kangaroos in a park at Margaret River, a region south of Perth, known for its vineyards and gastronomy.

Here's a chance to see some notable shipwrecks, most notably the wooden hull of the 544-metric-ton (600-ton) **Batavia**, flagship of the Dutch East India Company, which went aground in 1629 and was salvaged and restored in the late 20th century.

The **Fremantle History Museum,** at the other end of town, occupies yet another convict-built complex. It first served as a lunatic asylum for deranged prisoners, then a training center for midwives, later an old women's home, and in World War II it found new life as a headquarters of the US Navy. Now demobilized and brightly restored, the Colonial Gothic building houses exhibits on the history of Fremantle and its people.

If you're visiting Fremantle on the weekend, check out the lively **markets** on the corner of Henderson Street and South Terrace, from 10am or 11am to 5pm.

Rottnest Island

Don't be put off by the name: there is nothing rotten in the state of Western Australia, and certainly not on Rottnest Island. Even in the original Dutch, the name does the island no justice. Apparently, Commodore Willem de Vlaming, who landed here in 1696, confused the indigenous quokkas (a sort of undersized wallaby) with some imaginary species of rat. So he called the island Rottnest, or rat's nest. In spite of this unkind mistake, the Dutch explorer considered Rottnest an earthly paradise. And you'll probably agree.

A good reason for going over the sea to Rottnest (18 km/12 miles from Fremantle) is to see the fetching little quokkas, with babies in the pouch like their kangaroo cousins. Other attractions are peacocks and pheasants, which were introduced when the governors of Western Australia used the island as a summer residence. And you can spot dozens of other species of birds, including the curlew sandpiper, the red-necked stint, and the osprey. Since 1941 the island has been a wildlife sanctuary, where it's forbidden to tamper with any of nature, even the snakes.

Rottnest is as quiet as an idyllic, barefoot sort of isle ought to be. The number of cars is severely curtailed. Bicycles are the most popular way of exploring the 40 km (25 miles) of coastline. Look into the swimming, snorkeling, fishing, and boating opportunities.

Four ferry operators serve Rottnest (nicknamed "Rotto" by Aussies) from Perth or Fremantle. It's an 80-minute cruise from Perth; double that from Fremantle. You can fly there in 20 minutes.

Excursions Inland

Just to the east of Perth, the **Darling Range** is the beginning of the great inland plateau. Amid the tall trees and colorful wildflowers are lookout points for views of the city and the sea. Waterfalls, brooks, and dams refresh the relaxing scene.

The **Swan Valley,** only about half an hour's drive northeast of Perth, is a high-priority destination for wine lovers. The area is noted for its small, family-run vineyards. The wine-making tradition in the Swan Valley dates back to the foundation of Western Australia. If wine tasting and driving seem incompatible, you can take a coach tour of selected vineyards, or the even more popular river cruise with stops at one or two wine cellars.

Farther east, the green expanse of the **Avon Valley** provides pastureland for cattle and grows the grain to feed Perth and beyond. The colony's first inland settlement, York is proud of its history. More than a dozen 19th-century buildings have been restored; several now serve as museums. Just outside town, one of the early farms has been restored to a "living museum" in which you can watch blacksmiths and wheelwrights at work. Clydesdale horses still plough the fields.

The nearest national park to Perth, **Yanchep** is known for its eucalyptus forests, its wild flowers, and a series of limestone caves. There is also an island-studded lake called **Loch McNess,** named after a local philanthropist, Sir Charles McNess. But don't bother looking for a Loch McNess monster. You can, however, see a koala colony here.

Natural Wonders

 A spectacle reckoned to be more than 2.5 billion years old is **Wave Rock** — one of those natural phenomena worth a long detour. And it will probably require one — it's a 700 km (437 mile) roundtrip drive from Perth. The rock stands near the small town of **Hyden,** about 350 km (217 miles) inland from Perth, in the wide-open spaces where the wheat, oats, and barley grow. The rock itself takes the form of a stupendous surfer's wave, as tall as a five-story building, eternally on the verge of breaking. Walking under the impending splash is one of the state's most popular tourist activities. Energetic visitors can also climb to the top. Other extraordinary rock formations in the area have expressive names like Hippo's Yawn and The Humps.

In **Nambung National Park,** about 250 km (155 miles) north of Perth, the rocky marvels take the form of myriad limestone pillars jutting like stalagmites from the desert floor. Standing as high as 5–6 m (16–20 ft), the Pinnacles are scattered over perhaps a thousand acres.

Pevelly Beach, Margaret River, an area of outstanding natural beauty, featuring many visitable limestone caves.

Collectors' Rocks

An opal is simply hydrous silica, a jumble of submicroscopic crystals with little to commend it except its beauty. Diamonds, after all, are not only a girl's best friend but can be used for industrial purposes. But opals are good for nothing except jewelry.

Opals come in many colors: white, yellow, green, blue, red, or black. The highly prized black opals come from Lightning Ridge, New South Wales. Coober Pedy is best known for its white or milky opals. In 1956 an opal weighing 7½ pounds was unearthed at Coober Pedy. The price was A$1.7 million.

The imagination runs wild. The park entrance is located near the lobstering village of Cervantes.

The Southwest

Excursions to the southwestern corner of the state encompass a delightful variety of scenery: beaches, vineyards, orchards, and soaring **jarrah forests.** Where the water table is high, you'll see stands of paperbark trees; you could strip off a layer of the papyrus-style bark and write a letter. But the most impressive tree in the region is the jarrah, a giant variety of eucalyptus. The lower half grows straight and clean as a telephone pole, with all the branches emerging at the top. Less than 10 percent of Western Australia's original old-growth forests are still standing, but the state's new Labor government, which came to power in February 2001, have pledged to protect all of it from logging to safeguard the future of eco-tourism in the state. So the forests will still be there when you arrive.

Bunbury is a pleasant vacation town in the southwest. You can swim with the dolphins at Koombana beach there. The **Margaret**

River region, an area between Cape Naturaliste and Cape Leeuwin, is honeycombed with limestone caves, some of which are open to the public. South of **Dunsborough, Yallingup Caves** are a fantastic underground world of elaborately carved limestone. Check with the local tourist office for details.

Margaret River lies at the heart of the state's top wine-growing and gourmet dining region. Specialties include brie, fresh berries, and marron (freshwater shellfish), while accommodations range from boutique guesthouses to five-star hotels or campsites under a million stars. Enchanting little places to stay include Cape Lodge, built in South African Cape style. Relaxing yet elegant, this is the perfect location from which to tour noted vineyards including Cape Clairault, Leeuwin Estate, Cape Mentella, Sandalford, and Vasse Felix.

Broome, a seaport town with a heavy Asian influence, once supplied most of the world's mother-of-pearl.

The Goldfields

 Kalgoorlie, about 550 air km (341 miles) east of Perth, retains the atmosphere of the riotous gold-rush town it was in the 1890s. The streets, laid out in a grid, are wide enough for stagecoaches or camel trains to U-turn. Like a Wild West movie set, there are verandahed saloons for every occasion. Optimists still scan old worked-over sites in search of forgotten nuggets. The occasional whopper still turns up.

The first big strike of Kalgoorlie gold came in June 1893, when an Irishman named Patrick Hannan stumbled onto enough glitter to really shout about. Paddy Hannan has never been forgotten in Kalgoorlie. A bronze statue of the bearded prospector adorns the main street, which bears his name; a replica of the water bag he carried serves as the municipal water fountain.

The almost total lack of water was the first desperate hardship to face the thousands of prospectors who rushed headlong into the goldfields when Hannan's news spread. Disease and death by dehydration took a heavy toll. The solution was found by another Irishman — an engineer named C.Y. O'Connor who constructed a 560-km (347-mile) pipeline from a reservoir near Perth. You can still see the big above-ground pipes by the side of the road. Wounded by criticism of the project, O'Connor killed himself before the first drop of water reached Kalgoorlie; he is now honored by a statue on the waterfront in Fremantle.

As the prospectors came in from the surrounding desert with their sudden wealth, Kalgoorlie turned into a rip-roaring supplier of wine, women, and song. The pubs were legion; many still retain their frontier atmosphere. Another old mining tradition is the red-light district of Hay Street, although at last inspection only three of the notorious "tin-shack" brothels were still in business. You can gauge how prosperous the town was from the elegance of the Victorian buildings, most notably in the three-story arcaded headquarters of the **Museum of the Goldfields.** This institution is stacked with exhibits detailing the life and work of those early prospectors. As for gambling, the town doesn't have a casino, but 7 km (4.5 miles) out in the country on the Menzies Road "Australia's only legalized **bush two-up school**" flourishes from midday to sundown. Just follow signs marked "Two Up."

Hannan's North Tourist Mine is a former mine converted for tourism use. You can take a 40-minute journey underground. Ex-miners conduct the guided tours and it's most interesting — although most people are delighted to see daylight again.

A ramshackle train called the Rattler (for obvious reasons) makes a one-hour loop around Kalgoorlie's Golden Mile twice daily, departing Boulder station at 10am and 12:45pm. **Boulder,** by the way, is Kalgoorlie's neighboring (and slightly shabbier) twin town.

A year before Paddy Hannan's big strike at Kalgoorlie, gold was discovered at **Coolgardie,** 40 km (25 miles) west of Kalgoorlie. Today Coolgardie proudly bears the slogan of "ghost town"; in fact, ghosting is its principal industry, and if there's a bit of melancholy in the air, it can only be good for business. The historical markers here seem to far outnumber the population, which by the turn of the century was 15,000.

Any good ghost town needs an interesting cemetery, and the inscriptions on the headstones in Coolgardie's graveyard tell revealing stories of the harsh frontier life. Among the Afghani camel drivers buried here, at least one is listed as having been murdered.

The Kimberley

More than 1,500 km (more than 930 miles) north of the gold lode, one of the richest diamond mines in the world gives a sparkle to the rugged, remote Kimberley region of Western Australia.

The **Argyle mine** produces a sizeable heap of exquisite pink diamonds — a coveted rarity in the gem world — as well as vast quantities of industrial diamonds that are used for grinding and drilling. Machines beside which mere humans look like Lilliputians move

Dinosaur footprints exposed by low tide at Gantheaume Point, Broome.

the ore along to the Argyle processing plant, where millions of carats per year are yielded.

The Kimberley, a dramatic, elemental, and spectacular area of waterfalls, thunderstorms, searing heat, and torrential rain (the latter two depending on season), is thought to hide as many as half of all the diamonds on earth. But that's not its only distinction.

More than three times the size of England, the Kimberley has fewer people per square kilometer than almost anywhere else in the world. The enormous region is known for Aboriginal rock art, including the mysterious **"Bradshaw figures,"** named after explorer

Joseph Bradshaw, the first European to describe them. In 1891, Bradshaw wrote: "The most remarkable fact in connection with these drawings is that wherever a profile face is shown, the features are of a most pronounced aquiline type, quite different from those of any native we encountered. Indeed, looking at some of the groups, one might almost think himself viewing the painted walls of an Egyptian temple." The drawings are believed by scholars to have derived from an unknown culture that flourished sometime before 15,000 b.c. — long before the Egyptians had built their temples.

Until a few decades ago, the Kimberley was the domain of intrepid explorers. It has been opened up since, with tour operators using four-wheel-drive vehicles, boats, helicopters, and small aircraft to reach far-flung attractions: towering gorges on the Fitzroy River; **Purnululu (Bungle Bungle) National Park** with its orange-and-black beehive-striped mounds; the sandstone and volcanic country of Prince Regent Nature Reserve; the tidal "waterfalls" near Derby; and eerie **Wolfe Creek Crater Meteorite Reserve.** The meteorite crater is 850 km (528 miles) across. Aborigines call the area "Kandimalal," which means "the place where the snake emerged from the ground."

On the coast, the seaport of **Broome** has a romantic past. It once supplied 80 percent of all the world's mother-of-pearl. Divers from Japan, Malaya, and the Philippines went out on 400 boats, diving for oysters and the pearls within them. The Asian aura still lingers, even if the mother-of-pearl business died with the introduction of cultured pearls and plastic buttons. You will find evidence of past glories in **Chinatown**, in the old Japanese boarding houses, and in the gambling and other pleasure palaces —all reminders of the port's early 20th-century heyday. The main attraction today is **Cable Beach**, a fantastic 22-km (14-mile) stretch of golden sands. At **Gantheaume Point**, low tide exposes dinosaur footprints about 130 million years old. If you stay late on the beach in March/April or August/September you may be lucky enough to see a natural phenomenon called "the Staircase to the Moon," an illusion caused by the full moon reflecting on mud flats at extreme low tide. It can be seen from the jetty during the king tides in those months.

SOUTH AUSTRALIA

The state's official animal symbol is the hairy-nosed wombat, but don't let that put you off. This shy native of South Australia is just as cuddly as any koala (if rather heavier); it is merely lacking the services of any public relations advisers to polish up its image.

Like the amiable wombat, South Australia is self-reliant. Everything the state needs can be found within its borders: coal from the open-cut mines of Leigh Creek, gas under the northeastern desert, grain and cattle through hundreds of miles of latitude, fish from the Southern Ocean, and world-renowned wines from scenic vineyards. South Australia produces more than 70 percent of Australia's wine.

The sights of South Australia are as many and varied as its resources: with the rugged grandeur of the Flinders Ranges, the sand dunes of the north, the green banks of the Murray River, and the surf of the Great Australian Bight.

The history of South Australia is distinctive. Nothing quite so gross as convict settlers here; the colony was founded as a planned community run by wealthy idealists. The "free settlers only" tag is a source of local pride. Sobriety and morality were key-

Colorful Rundle Mall in downtown Adelaide.

Rowing practice on the River Torrens, which splits Adelaide between the business district and the residential area.

stones of the master plan, giving rise to a reputation for stuffy puritanism. Fortunately, the influence of the state's "wowsers" (bluenoses or killjoys) has long faded. For example, Maslin Beach just outside Adelaide became Australia's first legal nude beach.

In some social respects, South Australia has led the rest of the country. It was first to grant votes to women, first to appoint an Aboriginal governor and first to appoint a woman governor. Spread out across a million sq km (386,100 sq miles), the state occupies one-eighth of the entire continent. But because most of the state is unendurable desert, the inhabitants number only about one-twelfth of

Australia's total population. And most of these may be found living contentedly in the graceful capital city, Adelaide.

Adelaide

Adelaide is easy to reach. Its international airport is efficient, land transport links are good, and the city offers a cheerful introduction to Australia. Adelaide's sunny climate beams on the city's many parks and gardens, as well as its elegant squares and broad boulevards.

Although the population is just over one million, Adelaide is a relatively sophisticated capital, where culture and good living are important elements of the local scene. There is a significant art gallery and the world's largest collection of Aboriginal artifacts in the South Australian Museum. Every other year (even-numbered years) the city puts on a world-acclaimed international festival of the arts and a concurrent fringe festival. In the intervening, odd-numbered years, you can enjoy Womadelaide in February, a music festival with indigenous musicians from around the world.

Every day, the locals here pay tribute to international culinary art, dining out in hundreds of excellent restaurants. Chefs work with excellent raw material. You can see and taste it at the **Central Market** in Gouger Street — fresh produce from all parts of the state, including McLaren Vale olives, Coffin Bay oysters, Barossa mettwursts, and Riverland dried fruits.

Nightlife encompasses rock concerts, nightclubs, discotheques, strip shows, and a casino. The city has come a long way since the days when outsiders joked, "I went to Adelaide once but it was closed."

Adelaide was founded two generations after the settlement of Sydney, in the reign of King William IV, and named after his queen, the former Princess Adelaide of Saxe-Meiningen. Although the southern coastline had been well charted, the idea of building a city beside the Torrens River didn't catch on until the 1830s. Before the first earth was turned, the city was planned on paper, street by street and park by park. The business district covers the area of 2½ sq km

(1 sq mile), precisely. The model, with its built-in green belt, was a winner, and so it remains.

City Sights

The most stately of streets in Adelaide, a considerable superlative here, is North Terrace, which delineates the northern edge of the business district. **North Terrace** is lined with trees and distinguished buildings — mansions and museums, churches and memorials.

Between the Terrace and the gently sloping, landscaped bank of the river is the **Adelaide Festival Centre,** which calls to mind Sydney's Opera House, but with angular planes in place of billowing curves; Adelaide also managed to truncate Sydney's lavish price tag. The relatively budget-priced, $20-million complex has a theater for every occasion. The 2,000-seat Festival Theatre (Australia's largest) is convertible, in three hours, from an opera house to a concert hall with outstanding acoustics. A drama theater seats some 600 people, an experimental theater, 350. There are hourly backstage tours of the establishment and a theater museum preserves South Australia's rich history and interest in the performing arts. Outside, bold sculptures are strewn around the plaza. You can eat outdoors in a Festival Centre bistro overlooking the river, or make your own picnic on the lawn. Or take a sightseeing boat up the river to the zoo, where you can pet the kangaroos and admire an outstanding collection of Australian birds.

Just behind the Festival Centre, **the South Australian Parliament House** is dignified by 10 Corinthian columns and so much expensive stonework it earned the nickname of the "marble palace." The foundation was laid in 1881 but work continued, on and off, over the following 58 years. Next door, the **Constitutional Museum** occupies the former Legislative Council building. It's Australia's only museum of political history.

A startling change of pace lies in ambush just next door: **Adelaide Casino** is situated in a dazzling conversion of the vastly

Relaxing in the sun on Glenelg Beach, Adelaide, on the Indian Ocean.

cupolaed old railway station. They've created a wonderfully plush gambling den which, with its potted palms, marble floors, and mighty chandeliers, is open to ordinary people (from 10am to 6am over the weekend, and otherwise until 4am). The visitors seem to prefer keno, a bingoesque game, to the complexities of blackjack, roulette, baccarat, and other international pastimes offered.

Elsewhere along North Terrace, the **University of Adelaide** is at the heart of a cluster of cultural institutions. Whale skeletons fill the show windows of the **South Australian Museum** as an alluring invitation. Inside is a monumental collection of Aboriginal arti-facts. A striking large-screen video display relates the story of the Aboriginal Dreamtime hero Ngurunderi. Other countries are well represented in a comprehensive survey of ceremonial masks, shields, and sculptures from South Pacific islands. And you can see a traditional trading vessel from New Guinea, which remained in service until recent times, with a bamboo deck and a sail made of bark. The museum also features a didactic display of stuffed Australian animals, reptiles, birds, and fish.

The **Art Gallery of South Australia,** which officially opened in 1881, covers many centuries of the world's art, and ranges from ancient Chinese ceramics to contemporary Australian prints, drawings, paintings, and sculptures. There's an extensive collection of Aboriginal art.

Two more historic buildings on North Terrace are **Holy Trinity Church,** the first Anglican church built in South Australia (begun in 1838), and **Ayers House,** a 45-room mansion furnished in an opulent 19th-century style. The house was owned by a local businessman and statesman, Sir Henry Ayers, after whom an admiring explorer named Ayers Rock.

Parallel with North Terrace is **Rundle Mall,** an all-weather pedestrian mall, and the heart of Adelaide's shopping area. Its trademark is a sculpture comprising double-decked spheres of stainless steel reflecting the animation all around. The mall's merchants include department stores, boutiques, cafés, and restaurants, all enlivened by street entertainers. The **Myer Centre** includes the city's two best department stores (along with a futuristic amusement area called Dazzleland), and Rundle Mall boasts Adelaide's two best pubs, the Exeter and the Austral. Rundle Street (the eastern extension of Rundle Mall) is an artsy and pleasant quarter. The westward extension of Rundle Mall, Hindley Street, has clubs and live entertainment, amusement arcades, even strip clubs.

Located on Grenfell Street is **Tandanya,** an Aboriginal cultural center offering art galleries, a workshop, and performing arts. The shop there is a good place to buy authentic Aboriginal souvenirs.

North of the city center, **Light's Vision** is not a sound-and-light show, as its name may suggest. It's a monument to the foresight of Lieutenant-Colonel William Light, who was sent out in 1836 to find

Barossa Valley vintners produce some of Australia's finest wines, enjoyed around the world.

the ideal site for a model city, then devise the total plan for its development. Atop a pedestal on **Montefiore Hill,** his statue peers over the parklands, pointing at the city of Adelaide, which he created.

Nearby Places

Adelaide has an outstanding public transport system, including the highly efficient O-Bahn, a "bullet bus" that steers itself along its own smooth roadway at speeds of up to 100km/h (over 60mph). It's billed as the fastest suburban bus service in the world. But nostalgia persists: The last surviving tramcars still clatter along between the edge of Victoria Square and the seashore at suburban Glenelg. This old-fashioned beach resort, from which a fishing pier forges far out to sea, was the original landing place used by the colonists who founded South Australia. A full-size replica of their vessel, a converted freighter named *H.M.S. Buffalo,* moored nearby, is now a museum and restaurant.

Among other beaches near Adelaide, from north to south along the Gulf of St. Vincent, you will find Semaphore, Grange, Henley Beach, West Beach, Somerton, Brighton, and Seacliff.

To the south and east of the city, the **Adelaide Hills,** the last manifestation of the Flinders Ranges, provide a background of forests, orchards, and vineyards. There are pleasant drives, walks, views, and picnic possibilities. The highest of the hills, **Mount Lofty** (770 m/2,526 ft) is only half an hour out of town by car. You can look down on the hang-gliding enthusiasts riding the hot air currents on the leisurely route back to sea level.

Hahndorf, a hill village situated about 30 km (19 miles) southeast of Adelaide, has changed little since it was settled in 1839 by German refugees. To the delight of sightseers, many of the original buildings in this oldest surviving German settlement in Australia have been restored. A number of folklore events brighten the tourist calendar, especially the Founders Day Festival, a marksmanship and beer-drinking celebration every January, and St. Nicholas Night in December.

Up the River

When it comes to the **Murray River**, Australians seem to go into rapturous delight. Having few rivers, they are thrilled by the local equivalent of the Mississippi. The Murray begins life in the Snowy Mountains (the Australian Alps), becomes the frontier between Victoria and New South Wales, and enjoys its last meandering through the state of South Australia. It is the river that accounts for the beautiful vineyards, orchards, and pastures along the way, not to mention the boating, fishing, and waterskiing. In the 19th century the river was a main highway for passengers and cargo, but

The lush Barossa Valley wine region, from Mengler Hill.

the advent of railroads and highways left the Murray more of a pleasure route.

Paddle steamers churn up nostalgia along the lower Murray, only an hour's drive from Adelaide. A variety of boats — big and small, ultra-modern and old-fashioned — offer short excursions or voyages of several days. It's also possible to hire a houseboat and ply the river at your own pace, in which case you can fish for your own dinner. The Murray cod run to gargantuan sizes, and you can change your diet by catching "yabbies," the big freshwater crustaceans akin to crayfish.

👉 Barossa Valley

Australia's best-known wine-producing region, the Barossa Valley, is also the prettiest. The scenery is a touchingly beautiful landscape of soft hills, sheep-grazing land, cozy villages, and the rows of vines that produce some famous wines. The Barossa's 45 wineries produce about a quarter of Australia's total vintage. The valley is easy to explore: just 30 km (19 miles) long by 14 km (9 miles) wide. Accommodations range from luxurious colonial mansions (with dinner, bed, and breakfast) to historic settlers' and miners' cottages, small motels, and fully serviced caravan and tent sites.

Barossa was founded by Germans who arrived in 1842 fleeing religious persecution at home. The Germanic atmosphere became a real liability when Australia plunged into World War I. Some of the Teutonic place names were changed for "patriotic" reasons, and the government shut down a German printing house in fear that subversive leaflets would be produced.

Nowadays, the Germanic atmosphere pervading the valley is part of the charm. You'll see neat stone cottages with filigreed verandahs and decorous gardens; if the inhabitants came out wearing *lederhosen* it wouldn't be much of a shock. You'll get to taste bratwurst and sauerkraut to the tune of oom-pah-pah music.

The Barossa Valley is only about an hour's drive northeast of Adelaide, a perfect distance for an easy all-day excursion devoted to sniffing out the local color and sampling the wines. Many of the wineries here are geared to this transient trade, advertising guided tours of the premises and offering explanatory tastings. The vineyard route is so popular that the roads and cellars can get crowded on Sundays and bank holidays.

Every other year (the odd numbers) the Barossa Valley stages an ebullient Vintage Festival in March or April, a week-long carnival as earthy as the wines to be celebrated. The locals — and thousands of visitors from Australia and overseas — dance in the streets, sing, play games, eat, and do a fair bit of drinking.

Kangaroo Island

South Australia's favorite escapist resort, Kangaroo Island is so big you could spend a week finding the best places for swimming, fishing, and sightseeing. About 145 km (90 miles) long and 30 km (19 miles) wide, it's the country's third largest island, after Tasmania and the Northern Territory's Melville Island. For tourists in a typical rush, though, there are one-day excursions; it's only half an hour by air from Adelaide.

The explorer Matthew Flinders, who circumnavigated Australia at the beginning of the 19th century, chanced upon Kangaroo Island in a storm. His hungry crew, amazed to be met by a mob of fearless, friendly kangaroos, consigned some of the reception committee to the stew pot. Grateful for the sustenance, the great navigator named the place Kangaroo Island. Right behind the Flinders expedition came a French explorer, Nicolas Baudin. Despite having lost the territorial claim to the British, he contributed some French names to the island's features. They're still on the map: places like D'Estrees Bay, Cape Du Couëdic, and Cape D'Estaing. Later settlers acknowledged Baudin's effort and built a white-domed monument to him at Hog Bay, called **Frenchman's Rock.**

The capital of Kangaroo Island, **Kingscote,** has a permanent population of about 1,450. Its elongated pier is where the car ferry coming from Port Adelaide docks; the island's airfield is only a few kilometers inland. Dolphins and seals frolic just off shore.

In 1919 the western end of the island was designated a nature reserve. **Flinders Chase National Park** is South Australia's biggest. Technically this is not a zoo; the animals are in their natural state, but in the absence of predators the kangaroos, koalas, and emus have become extroverts, trying to sponge or steal some food from the visitors.

On the south coast, Seal Bay belongs to Australian sea lions. They are so unafraid of humans that you can wander among them at will, except in certain fenced-off areas. Birdwatchers thrill to local species, which show clear differences from mainland relatives, and a noisy population of migratory birds from distant oceans.

Three Peninsulas

Just to the south of Adelaide, the **Fleurieu Peninsula** is an easy-to-reach, easy-to-like vacationland of surfing beaches, vineyards, and history. The history starts at the beginning of the 19th century when the French explorer Baudin named the peninsula after his navy minister, Count Pierre de Fleurieu. The first industry to be based on the peninsula was whaling, centered on **Victor Harbour.** It's now the area's biggest town, and a very popular year-round resort.

Yet another historic location is **Maslin's Beach** on the Gulf St. Vincent coast. Here a new leaf was turned in the evolution of Australian social customs. This was the nation's first legal nudists' beach. Now there are many to be found around the coastline.

Farther inland, scores of vineyards basking in the sunshine of the **Southern Vales** are the reason for the peninsula's fame. They've been making wine here since 1838, to great effect. Many of the wineries encourage connoisseurs or simply wine drinkers to stop in and try the vintages. The best-known area of wine production is **McLaren Vale.**

The **Yorke Peninsula,** west of Adelaide, first became important in the 19th century as a copper-mining district. Most of the region's miners were drafted in from Cornwall, England's copper-rich southwestern peninsula, and the Cornish touch can still be seen in the design of the old cottages and churches. Museums and the ruins of the mine superstructures provide constant reminders of the area's heyday, which continued until the 1920s. They've even kept up the homely tradition of baking Cornish pastries.

The **Eyre Peninsula** encompasses beach resorts, wheat fields, bushland, industrial centers, and a prized wilderness, the Lincoln National Park. Set atop magnificent cliffs at the tip of the peninsula, the park is home to kangaroos and birds as diverse as emus, parrots, and sea eagles. Fishing boats big and small are anchored in the attractive deepwater harbor of **Port Lincoln,** the tuna-fishing capital of Australia. Visit the home of the great white shark on a cruise to Dangerous Reef. Port Lincoln celebrates **Tunarama Free Festival** on the foreshore of Boston Bay each January over Australia Day weekend (26 January). Highlights include the World Record John West Tuna Tossing Championship, which sees world-class athletes turn up to throw tuna-fish. The record set in 1998 by Sean Carlin (who won gold for Australia in the hammer throw at the 1996 Atlanta Olympics, before switching to fish) still stands. Carlin hurled a tuna 37.23 m (122 ft), leaving awe-struck onlookers gasping.

The biggest city on the peninsula is **Whyalla,** which grew from a solid base of heavy industry — as heavy as iron and steel. If a blast furnace is your idea of fun, you can join one of the tours of the local steelworks (Mondays, Wednesdays, and Saturdays at 9:30am); the public is also able to visit the iron-mining area.

The Eyre Peninsula reaches as far west as **Ceduna,** where the limitless expanse of the **Nullarbor Plain** begins. It's more than 1,200 km (744 miles) from Ceduna westward to the next town of any significance (Norseman, WA). Filling stations do occur, but the route is lonely and grueling. Nullarbor is sometimes thought of as an Aboriginal word. It's actually Latin for "treeless," an indication that the plain is also waterless. But, as the Aboriginal inhabitants have always been aware, water is there if you know where to look for it: underground in limestone caverns. The highway follows the dunes and cliffs that lie along the length of the **Great Australian Bight,** which forms the bulk of the continent's curving southern coast.

☞ Flinders Ranges

For scenic splendor, South Australia's Outback competes well with the remote areas of the other states, nowhere more impressively than in the Flinders Ranges. Rising from a landscape as flat as the sea, the tinted peaks speak poetry to lovers of robust scenery. In the spring the rugged wooded hillsides come to life with a flood of wildflowers, but at any time of year the scene is intriguing. The mountains, like the desert, are much more colorful at close range.

An outstanding phenomenon found in the Flinders Ranges is a huge natural basin called **Wilpena Pound.** Rimmed by sheer cliffs, the saucer is approximately 20 km (12½ miles) long and 8 km (5 miles) wide. Wilpena Pound is not only spectacular as a scenic and a geological curiosity, it also wins admiring squawks from the birdwatchers. This is a place where you can spot species including butcherbirds, wagtails, galahs, honeyeaters, and wedge-tailed eagles.

The flat floor of the Pound is perfectly designed for bush walks (suggested routes are signposted). But not in summer, when it's altogether too hot for unnecessary exertion. In any season it's essential to carry a supply of drinking water. There's only one way into the amphitheater, through a narrow gorge occupied in rainy times by Wilpena Creek.

An area of such grandeur was bound to inspire Aboriginal myths and art over thousands of years. Timeless rock paintings can be inspected near Wilpena at **Arkaroo** and at **Yourambulla,** south of the village of **Hawker.**

Coober Pedy

The town the opals come from must rate as one of the most bizarre tourist attractions anywhere. When you say "desert" this is what it means: In the summer the daytime temperature can reach 45°C (113°F) to 50°C (122°F). That's in the shade, of which supplies are extremely limited. In the winter the nights become unpleasantly cold. Yet a couple of thousand people make their home in this far corner of the Outback.

The name Coober Pedy comes from an Aboriginal phrase meaning "white fellow's hole in the ground." Indeed, the settlers have survived here by burrowing hobbit-like into the side of a low hill. The temperatures within are constant and comfortable, regardless of the excesses outside. Among the dugouts are residences of some luxury, with electricity and wall-to-wall carpets. Also underground are a Roman Catholic chapel, a bank, and an air-conditioned motel.

Regular tours by bus or plane bring the curious crowds to Coober Pedy, about 950 km (589 miles) northwest of Adelaide. The tours visit the local opal fields, where most of the world's opals are produced, with demonstrations of opal cutting and polishing. Having learned the intricacies, you can buy finished stones and jewelry on the spot. Or try noodling in the mullock heaps: all you need is a rake or a sieve to sift through the rubble at the top of each mineshaft, and if you're lucky you may find an overlooked opal. But note that amateur fortune-seekers need a permit (obtainable from the Mines Department in Coober Pedy or Adelaide) to go fossicking.

VICTORIA

By Australian standards, the state of Victoria is a midget. About the same size as Great Britain, and barely bigger than, say, Minnesota, it is the smallest state on the mainland. But its nearly 4.8 million inhabitants give Victoria Australia's highest population density.

Two out of three Victorians live in the capital, Melbourne, a center for finance, industry, culture, and sports. The sophisticated city folk live within easy striking distance of the state's bushland and 19th-century boomtowns, the sea, the vineyards, and ski slopes. Some of the scenery is so rich and pretty that the state's first name was *Australia Felix* — Latin for bountiful or lucky.

Victoria was the earliest state to industrialize, but it's still a leading farming power as well — hence the nickname of "Garden State." This agricultural potential remained unexploited until the 1860s, after the state's gold rush fizzled. Unemployed ex-prospectors eagerly fanned out as farmers, working land they bought for one pound per acre. Immigrants in search of a figurative pot of gold followed in a steady flow that reached a tidal wave after World War II, with the policy of "populate or perish." This produced both curious ethnic pockets around the state and the cosmopolitan effervescence of a multicultural society within the dignified confines of the capital city.

Melbourne

Elegant parks and gardens splash green patterns across Melbourne's map, softening the rigors of its precise grid plan, and offering merciful breathing space on the edges of the city center's hubbub. This is a friendly city of *serious* buildings and imposing Victorian architecture.

Its air of distinction may have something to do with the fact that the city was founded not by prisoners (as was Sydney) but by adventurous free enterprisers with their own vision of success.

It's all so grand you might forget Melbourne's rough-and-tumble pioneering days. The gold rush broke out in Victoria in 1851, only a few months after the fever hit New South Wales. A gold strike at Ballarat so electrified the state that Melbourne itself risked becoming a ghost town; businessmen locked their offices or shops and rushed to the goldfields, and ships were abandoned by their gold-crazed crews. New immigrants rushing in to fill the gap lived in shacks and tents. Successful diggers, on their return to Melbourne, had so much money to dispose of that morals loosened considerably.

Melbourne skyline glitters as night falls and daily activities give way to evening frivolities.

Melbourne's Trams

Tramcars (streetcars) are as much a part of Melbourne's character as Victorian architecture and football madness. The new trams are sleek and comfortable, the old ones worthy as relics.

Keep well clear of these 63 ½-metric ton (70-ton) trams. To accommodate them, Melbourne traffic is organized in a somewhat eccentric way. Trams have the right of way at crossroads; at certain main intersections, if you want to turn right, you have to move to the left lane, wait for the trams to pass, and then for the light to change before turning right.

A burgundy-and-gold-colored City Circle tram runs a loop around central Melbourne every 10 minutes and is free. You can even dine on a tramcar if you like — the Colonial Tramcar Restaurant is a converted 1927-vintage tram which serves dinner and lunch, complete with white linen, silver service and onboard facilities.

The long-running rivalry between Sydney and Melbourne is incurable. Sydney thinks Melbourne is boring, Melbourne thinks Sydney is superficial. Sydney blasts Melbourne's climate, Melbourne ridicules Sydney's self-satisfaction. Generally, Melbourne (with a total population of about 3.5 million) seems to be on the defensive, for instance on the subject of the unpredictable weather; temperatures are subject to extremes. And as for Sydney's Opera House, Melbourne was determined to outdo it, but in a "warm and welcoming" way, avoiding what was pointedly called "self-conscious grandeur." The outcome of that particular rivalry was the Victorian Arts Centre, a promising security blanket for local self-confidence.

If Melbourne is staid, as Sydneysiders allege, you'd never know it from their sports mania. "Footy" — or high-scoring Australian

Rules Football — is the main attraction here. Cricket is also a passion. And as for the horses, the Melbourne Cup is so all-engrossing that the first Tuesday in November, when the race is run, counts as a legal holiday.

A decade or two ago, Melbourne was a city that emptied after dark. That has changed dramatically. Residents have moved back into the inner city, and the Central Business District now boasts cafés, bars, and nightclubs. Melburnians have something of a reputation as gourmets; before deciding which of the 3,000 or so restaurants to patronize they diligently compare them in the local epicure guidebooks.

City Sights

A pleasant aspect of Melbourne can be viewed from the level of the Yarra, the river embellishing the center of the city. On the last few miles of its journey to the sea, the Yarra plays host to freighters, pleasure boats, and rowing regattas. And it waters the gardens, reflects the skyscrapers, and invites cyclists and joggers to follow its course along pretty landscaped paths. For a look up at the skyline and a close-up of river commerce, take one of the cruise boats that leave from **Princes Walk** by **Princes Bridge.**

Aerial views over the river and the city point up the ample

One of Melbourne's handy trams wends its way through the city's streets.

acres of green (contrasting with yellow and russet leaves in autumn) in the parks and gardens in among the business-like blocks. The best vantage point is the observation deck on level 55 of Australia's tallest building, **Rialto Towers** on Collins Street. The view extends beyond **Westgate Bridge** to the west, the **Dandenong Ranges** to the east, and the shimmering expanse of **Port Phillip Bay** to the south. The observation deck, with a licensed café bar, stands 253 m (830 ft) high. A 143-seat theater there called Rialto Vision shows a 20-minute film.

An inescapable sight along the waterfront is the enormous **Crown Entertainment Complex,** housing the 500-room **Crown Towers Hotel** and **Crown Casino.** The casino, Australia's largest gaming establishment, offers (at last count) 350 gaming tables and 2,500 video gaming machines. The complex also houses an enormous spa covering an entire floor, decorated in a style one observer compared to "a set from a Charlton Heston Bible epic."

Southbank, a riverside shopping and strolling precinct, runs alongside. On the opposite bank is the Polly Woodside, a square-rigged sailing barque, recalling the adventurous days of the last century. Launched in Ireland in 1885, the restored ship is now part of a maritime museum.

Near the river, just south of the heart of town, an Eiffel Tower–style superstructure marks the modern **Victorian Arts Centre.** This airy silver, gold, and white spire rises from flowing curves suggesting a ballet dancer's tutu.

The first part of the complex to open, in 1968, was the **National Gallery of Victoria,** now a high-priority stop for art lovers from the world over. The big collection covers European and Asian art, old and new, and of course offers a comprehensive look at Australian painting and sculpture. Among the choicest items on show are a vast, anecdotal Tiepolo painting from the 1740s, *The Banquet of Cleopatra;* sculptures by Rodin, Henry Moore, and Barbara Hepworth; a first-class survey of classical Chinese porcelain; and a splendid sampling of Australian Aboriginal paintings. The Gallery,

the scene of more than 100 hangings. The death masks of the most famous prisoners are displayed, along with other penal memorabilia, such as a "lashing triangle," last used in the enlightened year of 1958. The best-known character on death row, Ned Kelly, the celebrated bushranger, was executed here on Melbourne Cup Day 1880. The jail displays the weird suit of improvised armor he was wearing when captured. And you can step inside the executive-sized cell that was his last residence on earth; it has a fine view of the gallows.

Melbourne Museum, largest museum complex south of the equator, opened in 2000. It includes Bunjilaka (an Aboriginal center), the Pasifika Gallery (Pacific artifacts), a Living Forest Gallery, a Science and Life Gallery, a Children's Museum, a theater and a range of performance spaces. The Australia Gallery houses an equine shrine: the taxidermist's version of Phar Lap — a chestnut gelding considered to be the nation's greatest racehorse, and still a national hero. Phar Lap won the 1930 Melbourne Cup by three lengths, but his heart suddenly failed in 1932, after he won California's Agua Caliente Handicap.

And now for something livelier. Melbourne's **Chinatown** centers on Little Bourke Street, to the east of Swanston Street. Special street lights and gates define the area, in which you'll find Chinese restaurants jammed shoulder to shoulder with cafés, a church, small factories, and exotic shops. The area has had a unique flavor since the gold rush days, when fortune-hunters from China crowded into this low-rent district before and after their efforts out in the bush. Chinatown today glows on the maps of local gourmets.

So does **Queen Victoria Market,** which sums up the bounty of Australian agriculture. Just about everything that grows can be found here, piled up in irresistibly fresh pyramids. It's as if the best fruit and vegetables had been borrowed from every market from Sweden to Sicily. The best time to take in the atmosphere is early in the morning, but note that Queen Victoria Market is closed on

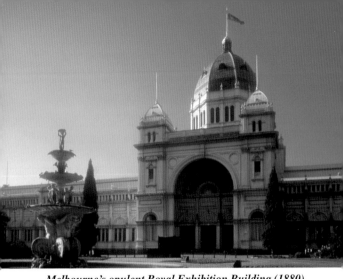

Melbourne's opulent Royal Exhibition Building (1880), recently restored, hosted Australia's first world exposition.

Mondays and Wednesdays. In addition to produce, you will find a flea market for cheap clothing and bric-a-brac.

Parks and Gardens

South of the river are the Royal Botanic Gardens, classed among the finest in the world. Thirty-six hectares (90 acres) of superb rolling landscape remind the visitor that Melbourne enjoys four seasons. Each time of year has its specialties, and seasonal leaflets are available for guide-yourself walks. For Australians, some of the joy of this park is the selection of brightly tinted trees and plants collected from the Northern Hemisphere. A total of 13,000 species are represented here, in addition to the lovely lawns and lakes.

Between the Botanic Gardens and Kings Domain stands the imposing Government House, the state governor's mansion, and La Trobe's Cottage, which is its early 19th-century predecessor. The timber cottage was shipped over from Britain to serve as a prefabricated home for Charles La Trobe, who became Victoria's first Lieutenant-Governor back in 1851. One of La Trobe's achievements was to establish a wine industry in Victoria.

Across from the cottage, the massive **Shrine of Remembrance** commemorates those Australians who fell in World War I; tragically, more than 60 percent of all Australian troops were either killed or wounded in the "war to end all wars." Once a year, every Armistice Day at 11am, a beam of sunlight coming through an opening in the roof strikes the Rock of Remembrance. It is a truly powerful and poignant experience.

In Parkville, north of the city center, the **Royal Melbourne Zoological Gardens** charm foreign visitors with kangaroos, koalas, platypuses, and the like, while amazing the locals with an all-star cast of elephants, giraffes, monkeys, and other animals from afar. In summer, musical entertainment is provided. The zoo is open 365 days a year from 9am–5pm.

Suburbs

The inner city suburb of Carlton combines the restored elegance of Victorian architecture with contemporary dynamism. The latter may be attributed to the area's immigrant colony, mostly Italian. Hence there is a great profusion of outdoor cafés, pizzerias, trattorias, and gelaterias.

In **South Yarra,** about 2 hectares (5 acres) of lawns and gardens surround Melbourne's finest stately home, **Como House.** Now run by the National Trust, this example of the colonial era's high style was completed with the addition of a gold-and-white ballroom in the 1870s. Each of its two stories was built with wide verandahs decorated with intricate ironwork.

Excursion boat at Southbank on the Yarra River, with Melbourne CBD in the background.

Toorak, the snootiest of suburbs, is rumored to harbor more money than any other suburb in Australia. The mansions, nicely landscaped, make tourists and most other passersby stand and gape. Shopping on Toorak Road is full of stylish delights.

A totally different shopping experience awaits in the seaside suburb of **St. Kilda.** On Sundays its Esplanade is taken over by artists, antiques dealers, and flea market entrepreneurs of every sort. Acland Street's restaurants, cafés, and bakeries preserve a middle-European Jewish flavor.

Lygon Street, **Carlton,** is Melbourne's slice of Italy, replete with pasta restaurants interspersed with wine bars, cheese shops, quality fashion boutiques, and delicatessens. Jimmy Watson's bar/restaurant in Lygon Street is a Melbourne institution.

Brunswick Street, **Fitzroy**, reflects the city's bohemian side. Restaurants and cafés, Spanish bars, comedy and live-band venues — all buzzing with activity day and night. Fitzroy's streets are crammed with alternative lifestyle shops, second-hand clothing, and funky furniture.

Excursions

A favorite day trip from Melbourne goes out to the **Dandenong Ranges,** volcanic mountains where flowered hillsides and eucalyptus forests set the scene for total relaxation. Only an hour's drive from town, the hills won't take your breath away; Mount Dandenong itself claims an altitude of only 633 m (2,077 ft).

One highlight of a day among the small towns, farms, parks, and gardens of the Dandenongs is a ride on **Puffing Billy,** a restored old steam train plying 13 km (8 miles) of narrow-gauge track. The line was given over to passenger operations from 1900 to 1958. Four years later it was converted to the tourism business. The train never achieves great speed. In fact, an annual race pits Puffing Billy against hundreds of runners.

The **William Ricketts Sanctuary** is an extraordinary collection of sculpture produced by a caucasion loner who was obsessed with Aboriginal culture and its near-destruction by his fellow whites. Ricketts carved incredibly lifelike faces of Aboriginal people, accompanied by their spiritual symbols. The result of his artistic toils is unorthodox, and may even be found unnerving.

In **Sherbrooke Forest Park** you can give your lungs a treat, savoring the elixir of ferns and mountain ash and whatever flowers happen to be in bloom. The forest is immensely tall, with mountain ash monuments as high as 20-story buildings and ferns as big as palm trees. This is the place to see, or at least hear, the lyrebird, a great mimic; it does imitations of other birds, human voices, and even of inanimate objects such as passing cars. Among the animal residents of the park is the echidna, alias the spiny anteater.

Healesville, less than 60 km (37 miles) to the east of Melbourne, is the place to go for an intimate look at Australian animals on their home ground. **Healesville Sanctuary,** nearby in the Yarra Valley, contains more than 200 native species, such as kangaroos, wombats, and emus. The animals feel quite comfortable mingling with the visitors, hoping to share a picnic. The sanctuary was founded in 1921 as a research establishment for the study of the local fauna, and is committed to the care of Australian wildlife and the conservation of endangered species.

The **Yarra Valley** was the site of the first commercial winery in the state, dating back to the middle of the 19th century. The region's vineyards are world-class; well worth a wine-tasting outing.

Penguin Parade

For a magical experience for both adults and children, try a long day-trip to **Phillip Island**, home of the fairy penguins (also known as little penguins), the world's smallest members of the penguin family. Hundreds of these engaging birds, standing about 40 cm (16 inches) high and looking quite formal in their blue-grey plumage with white fronts, come home at sunset; the number varies depending on activities at sea, where they spend most of their time fishing. For reasons of their own, perhaps sensing danger, they tread water offshore until night falls, when they venture onto the beach. After decades of being stared at by visitors, they still feel insecure arriving on the island.

Before dusk falls, hundreds of tourists gather behind ropes on Summerland Beach and in viewing platforms on the sandhills above. You're not allowed to do anything that might upset the penguins: no flash cameras, no running, no sudden movement. The penguins observe all this and wait for the first star to appear in the sky. The first brave penguin scout scrambles onto dry land and, suspiciously, lurches across the beach and up the hill to his burrow. In small groups the others follow, waddling through the sand dunes up to their burrows right at sunset, just as their ancestors have done night after night for thousands of generations. It can take half an hour or more for all the birds that are coming ashore to arrive.

Phillip Island, which is situated 120 km (74½ miles) southeast of Melbourne, receives about 2 million visitors a year. The visitor center here has a simulated underwater display where you can study the penguins' life at sea. The island is linked to the mainland by a bridge at San Remo. The penguins are the stars, but the supporting cast is also well worth seeing: thousands of fur seals residing on tall rocks on the west coast; clouds of mutton birds arriving each November from their wintering grounds thousands of miles away; and a colony of koalas, vegetating in the high branches of the gum trees. Take a sweater or coat for the penguin parade, for the nights are chilly even in summer.

Wilsons Promontory

Until the Ice Age, the southernmost tip of the Australian mainland was connected to Tasmania. When the ice melted the heights became an island. Since then the dunes have built up, linking the massive promontory to the rest of Victoria. The varied and spectacular scenery has made Wilsons Promontory the state's most popular national park.

The coastline ranges from magnificent granite headlands to peaceful sandy beaches. Walking trails wander through forests and moorland and flower-covered heathland. Koalas live here, as do kangaroos and emus. Known locally as "The Prom," the peninsula is about 240 km (149 miles) southeast of Melbourne.

About an hour's drive west of Wilsons Promontory, on Bass Highway, the **Giant Earthworm Museum** displays a bizarre

Skeleton of a blue whale in the newly opened Melbourne Museum, the largest museum complex south of the equator.

life-form that you probably won't encounter anywhere else. *Megasolides australis* is a giant gurgling earthworm native to this region. It's the world's largest terrestrial invertebrate. The worm's gurgling (the sound of its passage through the ground) is loud enough to interrupt human conversation on the surface. It's enough to ruin your lunch. The museum (part of a nature theme park called **Wildlife Wonderland**) explains the life-cycle of the worm. An average specimen grows to about 3 m (almost 9 ft) long and some grow to about 5 m (16 ft).

An interactive display in the earthworm museum allows you to walk through a mock-up of the worm's stomach and listen to the sound of its heartbeat and the flowing of its blood. You can also see the worms themselves.

The Goldfields

A drive of 113 km (70 miles) to the west of Melbourne takes you well over a century back in time to the attractive town of **Ballarat,** rich with all the atmosphere of Australia's golden age. This is real gold-rush country, and it is still a prize destination for tourists.

Ballarat has a bittersweet history. Gold was discovered in 1851, and thousands of miners trekked to the fields. The early arrivals simply scooped up a fortune, but latecomers had to work harder, following the ore ever deeper.

Almost from the outset the government collected a license fee from the miners. Many newcomers couldn't afford to pay a tax, so they tended to lie low when the license inspectors swooped. In the midst of growing antagonism between the authorities and the miners, charges of murder and official corruption pushed the diggers to revolt. In the Eureka Rebellion, Australia's first and only uprising, insurgent miners were besieged in their stockade. An uneven battle cost many people their lives, mostly diggers. The nation was stunned. The anguish endured for years, inspiring poets and politicians.

When peace returned to the goldfields, and many of the miners' grievances were answered, Ballarat went back to the business of making a fortune. In 1858 a group of Cornishmen came upon what they called the Welcome Nugget, which weighed in at an enormous 63,000 grams (2,026 ounces). It was eventually put on show in the Crystal Palace in London before being minted. Parallel with the discovery of wealth, Ballarat grew into a stately town where even art and good taste had their day.

To see what Ballarat was like in the 1850s, visit **Sovereign Hill,** an open-air museum re-creating the sights, sounds, and smells of the gold rush. Local folk, dressed in Victorian-era clothing, operate the old shops, post office, bakery, and printing office of what appears to be a real town. Tourists are invited to try their hand with a digger's pan, under expert instruction. The **Gold Museum** traces the history

Statue of Captain Cook, Fitzroy Gardens, Melbourne.

of the mineral since biblical times and displays notable nuggets and gold coins.

In the real Ballarat, the principal public buildings on the town's wide tree-lined streets are a long-lasting monument to the good old days. Some of those who got rich quick had the good taste to spend some of their money on the finer things. Hence the statues of mythological subjects in Carrara marble in the **Botanical Gardens,** and the admirable collection of early Australian art in the **Ballarat Fine Art Gallery.**

Another treat for nostalgia fans is the town of **Bendigo,** situated 150 km (93 miles) northwest of Melbourne. The town's unusual name is a very roundabout corruption of Abednego, the Old Testament companion of Shadrach and Meshach. In the 1850s, Bendigo Creek, running through the center of town, was besieged with panning miners.

The **Central Deborah Mine** is now a museum of 19th-century mining technology. From there you can take a "Talking" Tram, an antique vehicle rigged up for tourists on an 8-km (5-mile) historic itinerary. The last stop is the **joss house.** One curiosity of Bendigo was the size of the Chinese population. Chinese miners, who enjoyed less than harmony with their white neighbors, worshipped in a prayer house constructed of timber and handmade bricks. The remains that stand today are filled with relics of the early Chinese fortune hunters.

TASMANIA

If you thought of Tasmania as the last stop before the South Pole, you're right; the Antarctic expeditions actually take off from Hobart.

No matter what direction you're heading in, it's a staging post you will hate to leave. Tasmania's scenery owes more to solar than polar influences. Although snow covers the hills in winter, it's a verdant island enjoying a temperate climate. Summer even brings shirt-sleeve weather, and you can find palm trees as well as poplars and oaks for some shade.

Suspended 240 km (149 miles) to the south of southernmost mainland Australia, Tasmania is small only by the swollen standards of the continent. With an area of approximately 68,000 sq km (26,255 sq miles), it's bigger than Sri Lanka or Switzerland.

Tassie, as the state is familiarly known, calls itself the Holiday Isle and pushes tourism. Its early residents would have had a bitter laugh at that, interspersed with an oath or two, for the island used to be the place where the really incorrigible prisoners were sent. While humble embezzlers and petty larcenists were transported to Sydney, the batterers and escape artists tended to be tagged for Tasmania.

Early explorers happened upon Tasmania because it lies on the 40th parallel — the Roaring Forties, along which an unfailing westerly wind blows around the globe. Their sailing ships could hardly miss the place. But that's not to diminish the achievement of the Dutch navigator, Abel Tasman, who gets credit for discovering the island in 1642. He named it after his sponsor, Anton Van Diemen, governor of the Dutch East Indies.

The Dutch never saw a future for the island, and Britain eventually claimed it simply to cut out the French. Because of the cruel conditions inflicted on the British prisoners, Van Diemen's Land acquired a sinister reputation. The very mention of the name could send a shiver down

Coppermine town, built to exploit Tasmania's rich mineral resources, near its west coast city, Queenstown.

a sinner's spine. The transportation of convicts was abolished in 1852, and some three years later the name was changed to Tasmania in memory of its discoverer and to improve the state's image.

Since then, Tasmania has become something of a tourist paradise. One day, some brilliant entrepreneur may put it on the world map and the crowds will arrive. Until then, if you like wild scenery, open moors, rolling green hills, deserted beaches, Georgian architecture, temperate-climate forests, uncrowded towns, and open-hearted people, you could easily become a Tasmaniac.

Hobart

Everybody knows that Sydney Harbor is the exciting one, glamorous and instantly recognizable all over the world. Hobart is the lovable harbor, a perfect ocean port on a dreamy river, with soft mountains rising beyond. It might have been transplanted from quite another seafaring latitude, as brisk and tidy as Bergen or Helsinki.

You never know what kind of ships you'll see here: freighters from Singapore, floating fish factories from Japan, or yachts from distant islands — perhaps Britain or Bermuda. The arrival of an ancient sealer, whaler, or windjammer in the harbor would be right

Wiping out the Aborigines

When Van Diemen's Land was first settled, the island's Aboriginal people may have numbered between 3,000 and 7,000. These native Tasmanians were different from the indigenous mainland peoples, in looks and culture.

As the British seized the land and wiped out the animals and birds that the indigenous tribes needed for food, the Aborigines fought back with punitive attacks. Enraged, the white men retaliated with all the force at their disposal. The survivors of this pogrom were exiled to Flinders Island, an outpost best known for its shipwrecks. There, they joined a handful of Tasmanian Aboriginal women who had been abducted by British and American whalers and sealers and taken to the island to serve as concubines or slaves. Although there were belated efforts to protect the race, the last of the full-blooded Tasmanian tribesmen died in 1876.

The race was not entirely exterminated, however, as mixed-blood descendants of some of the exiles on Flinders Island have since moved to Tasmania and founded a flourishing Aboriginal movement there.

Aboriginal artifacts can be seen at the Tasmanian Museum on Argyle Street in Hobart.

Murchison's landscape is typical of a mining town.

in character. Sail power still matters here: Hobart's Constitution Dock is the goal line of the grueling Sydney-to-Hobart yacht race.

Hobart, Australia's second oldest capital city, has kept a powerful array of historic monuments, from stately official buildings to quaint cottages. Best of all, they're spic-and-span and still in use.

Another, more recent historical distinction: Hobart was chosen as the site of Australia's first legal casino. The **Wrest Point** complex grew into an all-round recreation center, topped by the almost inevitable provincial status symbol, a revolving rooftop restaurant. Gambling facilities have since spread throughout the rest of Australia.

With a population of around 194,000 (suburbs included), Hobart is small enough to get around and get to know, and as unsophisticated and satisfying as the local fish and chips.

City Sights

In this deepwater port, the ships come right into the center of town. The waterfront, always colorful, is the place to begin exploring the city on foot. You can watch crates of giant crabs and scallops coming ashore, and follow their destiny to the floating fast-food restaurants moored here. Just behind **Constitution Dock,** where the yacht races end, the late Victorian–era **Customs House** stands out as one of the

Activities come to a close as dusk descends on Waterman's Dock in Hobart, Tasmania.

city's most imposing sandstone monuments. It was built at the turn of the century on the site of one of the colony's oldest landmarks, the original customs house.

Also bordering the docks, **Salamanca Place** is a long row of sandstone warehouses from the 1830s, restored and proudly occupied by artisans' workshops, boutiques, and restaurants. On Saturday mornings, stalls selling various arts and crafts, knickknacks, flowers, and vegetables cover the cobblestones; jugglers, mimes, and minstrels perform and pass the hat.

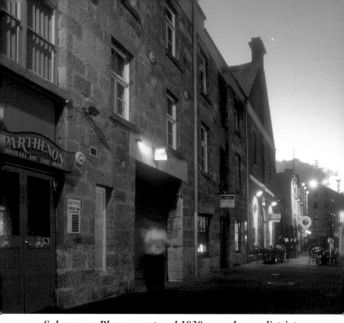

Salamanca Place, a restored 1830s warehouse district, now sports chichi craft shops and eateries, Hobart.

Altogether more serious is **Parliament House,** also facing the waterfront, built in 1840. The state's bicameral legislature operates in a low-rise stone building which displays some admirable architectural details.

Another venerable structure still in use is the **Theatre Royal** on Campbell Street, Australia's oldest live theater. Built in the most exquisitely luxurious style in 1834, it has featured stars like Noel Coward and Laurence Olivier.

Overlooking Salamanca Place, **Battery Point** is the historic heart of Hobart, beautifully preserved. The battery in question

174

was a set of coastal artillery guns installed in 1818. Ten years later signal flags were added, for relaying the big news of the day, such as ship arrivals or prison breaks. The area is worth an hour or two of exploration afoot, to absorb the atmosphere of the narrow streets, the mansions and cottages, churches and taverns. One of the upper-class colonial homes has been turned into the **Van Diemen's Land Memorial Folk Museum,** devoted to the colony's 19th-century way of life, and displaying artifacts from toys to farm equipment.

The **Tasmanian Museum and Art Gallery** is worth visiting for its collection related to the Tasmanian tiger (thylacine). This handsome, striped, dog-like marsupial is believed to have been hunted to extinction by the 1930s, although some people swear they have sighted living specimens in remote regions.

The center of Hobart is linked to the suburbs and the airport by the graceful **Tasman Bridge** across the **Derwent River.** The pre-stressed concrete bridge ran into trouble in 1975; more accurately, trouble ran into the bridge. A bulk ore carrier, off course, ploughed into the span of the bridge; tragically, four cars tumbled into the river and the ship sank.

For an expansive panorama of Hobart and the valley of the Derwent, ascend **Mount Wellington,** the city's most prominent landmark. It is named in appreciation of the Duke of Wellington, famous for toppling Napoleon at Waterloo. For this expedition you can forget your mountain-climbing equipment. A paved road goes all the way to Mount Wellington's summit, 1,270 m (4,167 ft) above the sea. Snow is a frequent visitor to the mountain in the winter months — an exciting novelty for tourists from more northerly Australian climes — but it rarely blocks the road.

Excursions from Hobart

A popular tourist destination up the river at Claremont is the Cadbury **chocolate factory**. Fans of Willy Wonka just love it — and guided

Cradle Mountain in Cradle Mountain Lake St. Clair National Park, Tasmania.

tours include as much chocolate as you can eat! The tours attract sweet-toothed visitors of all ages, but tots under eight must be carried.

Those without a sweet tooth might prefer touring the imposing **Cascade Brewery,** oldest in Australia, at 140 Cascade Road. The beer, made from pure Tasmanian water, is excellent. Cascade uses a Tasmanian tiger logo in its advertising and on its labels.

At **Taroona,** situated beyond Wrest Point, you can visit the remains, more than a century old, of a different kind of factory, the **Shot Tower.**

Though it looks like an ordinary smokestack, this tower 60 m (197 ft) tall was used in the manufacture of gunshot and musket balls. Molten lead was dropped from the top of the tower into cold water, and solidified in a perfectly spherical shape. You can climb the internal spiral staircase to the very summit for a view of the countryside.

A complex of modern office buildings at **Kingston** is the working headquarters for Australia's extensive operations in the neighborhood of the South Pole. The **Commonwealth Antarctic Division** coordinates logistics and research in fields such as glaciology, botany, physics, and medicine. Inside the main building are displays of sleds and faded flags from the early pioneering expeditions.

Launceston

Tasmania's second city is an agreeable, roomy town at the head of the Tamar River. Launceston exudes an unexpected English flavor, with

A quaint wooden home fits perfectly into the countryside scenery of Mole Creek.

Port Arthur, Australia's most brutal 19th century prison colony.

elm trees, rosebushes, and patriotic statues and plaques. The journey north from Hobart skirts soft green hills studded with sheep. In the villages, to enliven the scene, the houses have roofs the color of fire engines.

Launceston was founded in the year 1805 as Patersonia. Soon afterwards, the name was changed to that of the town of Launceston in Cornwall, which was the birthplace of the colony's governor. The historic aspects of the town are enthusiastically preserved, starting in the very center, the **City Square.** Here, challengingly grouped together, are a modern pyramid-style state office building, a Japanese garden, and a building from 1830, **Macquarie House.** Restored to mint condition, this sometime warehouse, barracks, and office building now serves as part of the local museum.

The main building of the **Queen Victoria Museum,** situated just a short stroll away on Wellington Street, has something for everyone, from stuffed platypuses to blunderbusses, from prisoners' chains to an invigorating collection of modern art. One surprising attraction here is an intact joss house which originally served the Chinese tin miners in the Tasmanian town of Weldborough. Downstairs, the Queen Vic Café is one of Launceston's best.

Life in early 19th-century Tasmania is recaptured at Penny Royal World. Here, a corn mill built in 1825 has been reconstituted, and a cannon foundry and arsenal created to demonstrate the stages of gunpowder manufacture, from the distillation of saltpeter to the finished cannonballs. Another attraction is the paddle-steamer Lady Stelfox. You can take a 45-minute ride on it.

Just around the bend is the Cataract Gorge, a stirring geological feature within walking distance of the center of town. Here the South Esk River slices between steep cliffs on its way to the Tamar. There are hiking trails, boating opportunities and, for sightseers who don't suffer queasy spells, a chairlift — the longest single-span lift in the world at 282 m (924 ft) — spans the canyon from on high.

Port Arthur

Tasmania's most visited historic highlight is the old penal colony of Port Arthur, an hour's drive from Hobart. Port Arthur's past is so grim, you'll be astonished at how picturesque it looks. Founded in 1830 as Australia's ultimate prison settlement, Port Arthur housed the most troublesome and intractable convicts — those who had committed second offenses after being transported to Australia. It rapidly became one of the world's most dreaded institutions, reputedly even more brutal than the French penal colony of Devil's Island in South America.

Chain gangs, toiling under the lash, built the solid stone buildings you see here today, which have survived more than a century of abandonment, fire, storm, and looting.

The biggest building still standing, at four stories high, was designed originally as a storehouse but became a penitentiary for 650 inmates. Other surviving buildings are the **Lunatic Asylum** (many prisoners went mad) and, next door, the "model" prison. Both have been restored. Convicts designed and built a large church, now in ruins. Its 13 spires represent Christ and the apostles. Then there is the mortuary, which did a lively business; more than 1,700 graves occupy the nearby **Isle of the Dead.** Other than by dying, Port Arthur was practically escape-proof, with sharks waiting on one side and half-starved killer dogs on the other. In total, some 10,000 prisoners did time at Port Arthur during its 47 years of operation.

As if that legacy of suffering wasn't enough, Port Arthur hit the headlines for the wrong reasons in 1996, when a maniacal visitor gunned down 53 men, women and children, killing 35, in the world's worst peacetime massacre.

Wilderness

For many Australians from the other side of the Bass Strait, Tasmania is the closest they can get to European-style scenery. At such a distance from Europe, though, the landscape is almost untouched by civilization. There is one good reason why it has remained unspoiled: it's often unapproachable by road. Four-wheel drive vehicles, canoes, rafts, or just sturdy legs are the best methods of penetrating these wild places. In Tasmania a higher percentage of the total area has been set aside as national parks than in any other state.

Even so, attempts by various commercial interests to log or dam unspoiled wilderness regions have triggered notable clashes with Tasmania's strong conservationist movement. According to the Wilderness Society of Tasmania, over 22,000 hectares (54,361 acres) of native forest were logged in the state in 1999, nearly two-thirds in pure, "old-growth" forest. In every Australian state other than Tasmania, the logging of pure rainforest has been banned. Fortunately, much Tasmanian forest remains, national parks proliferate, and the interests of conservation and responsible tourism — as opposed to those of the logging and wood-chipping industries — may yet prevail.

South West National Park covers nearly all of the southwestern corner of Tasmania, and contains a variety of spectacular scenery, including rugged mountains, glacial lakes, icy rivers, and forests of giant Antarctic beeches. One recent feature of the region is the new **Lake Pedder,** flooded to 25 times its natural size for a hydroelectric project. For better or worse, the controversial project brought the first roads to the area.

A few hours' drive northwest of Hobart is **Cradle Mountain–Lake St. Clair National Park.** Here you'll discover a savage wonderland, filled by mountain peaks and waterfalls, temperate rainforests, and clear lakes astir with trout. The wildlife is all around you: wallabies, possums, Tasmanian devils, and wildcats. If the Tasmanian tiger wasn't thought to be extinct, this would probably be the place to find one.

Mount Field National Park, just an hour's drive from Hobart, is popular in the winter as an easy-to-reach, no-fuss skiing area. In the summer months the heathlands beyond the giant forests burst into bloom, creating a carpet of alpine flowers, although some areas are covered with pesky thickets of horizontal scrub, a Tasmanian specialty. At the entrance to the national park is a village with the engaging name of National Park.

The Living Reef

When the conditions are just right — when the sea is clear, warm, and not too deep — the coral reef builds itself.

The reef is a living organism, the work of millions of minute polyps building on the skeletons of their ancestors. They grow into surreal formations, such as elkhorn, swaying seafans, or a wrinkled brain. The coral feeds on, and in its turn feeds, microscopic algae. These oxygen-producing algae support schools of theatrically tinted fish, like angelfish, butterfly fish, and red emperors. These beauties attract the whoppers that fishermen dream of.

WHAT TO DO

SPORTS

Sporting life in Australia is inescapable, from the dawn jogger puffing past your window to the football crowds celebrating late into the night with shouting, songs, and car horns. In a country so beautiful, and with a climate so benign, you'll be tempted to join the sporting crowds, either playing the game yourself or watching the professionals. Under the dependable sun, everything is possible, from skiing — on water or snow — to surfing to sailing.

Sports, it's often said, are a passion Down Under. You can measure their impact by the newspapers, with their comprehensive sports sections, and by the amount of live sports coverage and results on television and radio. If Australians are not playing a game or watching it, they're most likely betting on the result, or at least arguing about it.

In what other country could a racehorse be as revered as is Phar Lap, winner of the 1930 Melbourne Cup? When he died, after a heroic victory in the United States, flags flew at half-staff in Sydney. Today Phar Lap's body is the star attraction in Melbourne Museum's Australia Gallery, and his mighty heart is preserved at the National Museum in Canberra. The Melbourne Cup race itself brings the nation to a temporary halt as everyone tunes in to listen.

But sporting tastes have changed over time. More than a century ago, a guidebook gloomily reported that very little hunting was available around Sydney, except when "occasionally parties are made up for rabbit, wallaby, or kangaroo shooting." In 1903 the first car race was run in Australia. Three years later, daringly, surf bathing in the daytime became legal in Sydney. And waterskiing caught on in 1936. Australia won the Davis Cup in 1939. When Melbourne hosted the Olympic games in 1956, Aussie athletes seized 35 of the medals. The world was becoming aware of Australia as one of the foremost sporting powers, a nation of hardy, aggressive competitors who could become champions in fields as varied as tennis and swimming, cricket and golf.

In 1983, joyous delirium swept the nation when the yacht Australia II captured the America's Cup. At the 1996 Atlanta Olympics, Australia was more successful per head of population than any of the top 20 countries. In 2000, at the Sydney Olympics, Australia came fourth in the medal tally (after the US, Russia, and China). Australia very nearly came third — it scored 58 medals, against China's 59. Australia's Olympic achievement in out-performing countries like Germany, France, Britain, and Japan is even more remarkable considering its population — just 19 million.

Watersports

Australia's endless coastline provides enough beaches, coves, and ports to keep the nation in the swim all year round. If that isn't enough, there are lakes, rivers, and swimming pools, both Olympic-size and backyard versions. Watersports of every variety are here for the taking.

Swimming in the Indian Ocean, the Tasman Sea, or the Coral Sea is the sort of sport you'll long remember. But the surf can be as dangerous as it is invigorating. Most of the popular beaches are delineated by flags showing where it's safe to swim. Beware of undertow or shifting currents and always obey the instructions of lifeguards. Sharks are a problem in some areas. In 2000, there were three deaths from shark attacks in Australian waters, and five other, non-fatal, attacks. When a shark alert is sounded, beat a retreat to the shore and ask questions later.

In spite of their mild-sounding name, jellyfish are a serious seasonal danger, especially in the north; elsewhere there may be Portuguese men-of-war, sea snakes, or other silent menaces. Check locally before you put a foot in the surf. A final word of caution: Before you stretch out on the beach, make sure that you protect

Australia is unmatched for the variety of its watersports, but just relaxing on the beach is also a favorite pastime.

yourself from the sun, which is more powerful than you think. Light complexions are particularly vulnerable to quick, painful sunburn and worse.

Snorkeling brings you into intimate contact with a brilliant new world full of multicolored fish and coral. The sport requires a minimum of equipment — a mask and breathing tube and, optionally, flippers to expand your range of operations. Practically anyone can learn how to snorkel in a matter of minutes, and there is no great skill or stamina required.

Scuba diving with an air tank is the advanced version of snorkeling. The best place in Australia for scuba outings — and quite possibly the best place in the world — is the coral wonderland of the

Great Barrier Reef. Some of the resort islands are equipped for all the needs of divers, though you may have to supply your own regulator and demand valves. If you want to learn the sport, some resorts have weekly courses starting in the swimming pool or a quiet cove, and leading up to an Open Water Certificate. Elsewhere along Australia's coasts, some serious scuba divers devote themselves to exploring submerged wrecks.

Surfing. Yet another discovery by the intrepid Captain Cook, who came upon this sport in Hawaii. He wrote: "The boldness and address with which we saw them perform these difficult and dangerous manoeuvres was altogether astonishing..." It was nearly two centuries before the first world championships were to be held in Sydney. Surfing areas are marked by signs, flags, or discs. The best-known surfing zone in the country must be Sydney's Bondi Beach, but there are many other fine locations up and down the coast of New South Wales. Although Queensland's Surfers Paradise may be just that, many of the experts prefer the giant rollers farther north at Noosa. Victoria's most popular surfing area is around Torquay. On the west coast, there are easily accessible surfing beaches near Perth and Bunbury.

Boating. Visiting yachts and their crews will always get a warm Aussie-style welcome. At popular resorts, for instance along the Gold Coast or the Great Barrier Reef, sailboats and powerboats can be chartered, with or without a professional skipper. Inland, you can command a sailboat or a houseboat on the relaxing Murray River. Or you might just want to settle for an hour's rental of a pedal boat.

Fishing. You'll need a license to fish inland waters in some states, but the sea is free for all amateurs. Outstanding trout fishing is found in Tasmania and the Snowy Mountains. Seasons and bag limits vary with the district. As for game fishing, the challenge of the giant black marlin is best met off the northern coast of Queensland. If your catch weighs less than half a ton, it's polite to throw the little

Surfers from all over the world come to test their skill, challenging the beastliest of Australia's waves.

fellow back. Or settle for tuna, mackerel, or sailfish. Good deep-sea fishing is also found off the coast of Western Australia, especially at Geraldton, and in the Spencer Gulf, near Adelaide. In the north, a coveted game fish is the barramundi — a great fighter prized for its delicate flesh.

Sports Ashore

Golf. The landscaping may be foreign, the climate may be a better year-round bet than you're accustomed to, but the game's the same. Melbourne considers itself the nation's golfing capital, with championship courses like Victoria and the Royal Melbourne. All the cities have golf clubs; they often operate under exchange agreements with clubs overseas, or you may have to be introduced by a local member. With no formality at all you can rent a set of clubs and play at one of the public courses to be found in all the sizeable towns. Golf is also a popular spectator sport in Australia. The Australian Open takes place in November.

Tennis. Having produced so many illustrious tennis champions, Australia takes the game seriously. You'll find courts available in the towns and resorts; some rent rackets and shoes. If you're just watching, then join the crowd. The biggest throng ever to watch a Davis Cup match was counted in Sydney in 1954: more

Windsurfing has become a popular sport, and the Australian beaches are an excellent place to practice.

than 25,000 fans. The world's top tennis stars usually tour Australia in December and January.

Bowling (lawn bowls). All over Australia this leisurely sport finds men and women in cream-colored costumes, spending hours in the sun decorously bowling on the neatly trimmed grass. If you're a bowler you'll be able to find a game at almost any club.

Skiing. Although Australia does not claim to have invented skiing, fur trappers in Tasmania were getting around on something similar to skis in the 1830s. The season in the Australian Alps usually lasts from June to September, and sometimes into November, which should be inducement enough for skiers from the Northern Hemisphere. The best-known and best-equipped of the ski resorts in the Snowy Mountains include Thredbo Village, Perisher Valley, and Smiggin Holes (NSW) and Mt. Buller, Falls Creek, Mt. Hotham, and Mt. Buffalo (Victoria).

The "Footy" Craze

In Australia the subject of **football** is so vast and complex — for a start, four different kinds of football are played — that the stranger is likely to be left gasping on the sidelines. But since the country is crazy about it, at least a few definitions may be useful. Incidentally, whatever type of football is being discussed, the fans are likely to call it "footy."

The cricket matches at Lilac Hill in Perth are not to be missed.

Australian Rules Football was introduced in Melbourne in 1858. Its zone of influence is mostly Melbourne and the south, although the National League now has teams based in most major cities. The crowds, which may reach up to 100,000 and more, come out in September to watch the finals, which generate the excitement of an American Super Bowl or an English FA Cup Final. The sport, combining elements of rugby, Gaelic football, and other forms of the game, is characterized by long-distance kicks and passes and high scoring on an oversized but crowded field — with 18 players to a side.

Rugby League, the professional and international version of the sport, is played mainly in Sydney and Brisbane. It's a roughhouse game offering great physical challenges to the players, who are 13 to a side.

Camel rides at Cable Beach, Broome are a nice diversion.

Rugby Union, with teams of 15, is fast, rough, and engrossing to the fans. Players from private schools add a posh aura to the violence of the tackles.

Soccer is the oldest of the country's games. In Australia it has benefited from the more recent waves of immigrants, and most clubs have ethnic connections. While soccer commands the biggest and liveliest crowds in Europe and South America, its Australian audience is relatively restrained.

More Sports To Watch

The Australians have been playing **cricket** since the early days of the penal colony at Sydney Cove. In its traditional form, the game goes on interminably — for as long as five days. Some years ago, responding to the television age, the Aussies had the temerity to make a show-biz spectacle out of a gentlemanly pursuit, playing at night under the lights in gaudy uniforms and ending the match decisively in a single day. Fortunately for conservative fans, the old-fashioned Test survives as well under the Australian sun. The season extends from October to the end of March.

Horseracing. Practically every Australian town, even in the Outback, has a race track, and the big cities tend to have more than one. The best times to go to the races are Saturdays and holidays. Betting on horses, or most other things, is as Australian as ice-cold beer. Enthusiasts who can't make it to the race track can participate in their own way through off-track betting facilities, legal and computerized and called TAB for Totalizator Agency Board. For punters who prefer to patronize illegal bookmakers, they are seldom far away.

The biggest race of the year is the Melbourne Cup, a 2-mile classic, followed so obsessively that the day it is run — the first Tuesday in November — is a legal holiday in Victoria. This is just as well, for nothing would get done in any case.

Trotting (harness racing) can be seen in big cities and some provincial locations. In the capital cities the trotters run at night under floodlights.

Greyhound racing is another spectacle that draws crowds of bettors. Spurred to great speed by the unfulfillable promise of an artificial rabbit, the dogs usually run in the cool of the evening; the audiences here can be as fascinating as the sport itself.

Motor racing. Big races take place near Brisbane, Sydney, and Melbourne. The biggest of all is the Australian Formula 1 Grand Prix in Melbourne, where you can watch the world championship contenders compete.

ENTERTAINMENT

Australia receives the best the world can offer in the performing arts, as well as producing masterpieces of its own. Open any major city newspaper for advertised performances of chamber music, opera, avant-garde plays, Aboriginal theater, comedy, cabaret,

Member of the Coffin Cheaters motorcycle gang, with his Harley-Davidson, Cable Beach, Broome.

Shakespearean classics, rock concerts, Broadway hits, dance, art shows, and touring exhibitions from the top galleries of Europe and North America.

Australia's two largest cities, Sydney and Melbourne, present the greatest number of cultural events, although Adelaide, in South Australia, hosts one of the most extensive and exciting — the Adelaide Festival, held biennially in even-numbered years.

Throughout the country, a lot of racy entertainment is available, as well as higher-brow cultural attractions such as opera, ballet, concerts, and drama. Between the extremes there's something for everybody who just wants a relaxing evening out.

Melbourne shines after dark— Australia's nightlife ranks with the best in the world.

In some smaller towns, odd events such as cane-toad racing, thong throwing (an open-toed sandal is hurled as far as possible), and brick-throwing draw the crowds. In coastal towns and cities, summer surf carnivals are another favorite — a chance for lifeguards to show off their skills, as well as a celebration of Australian beach culture.

Most towns have a "what's on" magazine or brochure listing details on the local agenda. In larger cities, daily newspapers run an entertainment section on Fridays or Saturdays.

Theater has been going strong in Australia for a couple of centuries. In 1789, scarcely a year after New South Wales was founded, a troupe of convicts put on a Restoration comedy (*The Recruiting Officer*) by George Farquhar as part of the celebrations for the birthday of King George III. The first real theater opened in Sydney in 1796. Drama today is at its liveliest in Sydney and Melbourne — mainly because their size ensures a reasonable audience — but you can enjoy performances in most cities.

Opera has attracted enthusiastic audiences Down Under since the days of Dame Nellie Melba. In more recent times, the coloratura brilliance of Dame Joan Sutherland spread her fame around the world. Seeing grand opera in the Sydney Opera House makes a gala occasion even more so; but opera-goers in other cities may enjoy better acoustics and atmosphere in their newer theaters.

Ballet and dance. The country's leading classical dance company, the Australian Ballet, founded in 1962, is based in Melbourne but performs in Sydney as well. Leading modern dance troupes include the Sydney Dance Company, the Australian Dance Theater, and the Bangarra Dance Theater. All varieties of dance have a following, from ballroom dancing (as seen in the Australian movie *Strictly Ballroom*) to tap-dancing (as depicted in the Australian movie *Bootmen*.)

Concerts. Every state and territory in Australia has its own symphony orchestra; many maintain youth and chamber orchestras as

Clowning musicians are among the myraid of buskers that provide entertainment at Southbank in Melbourne.

well. An influential promoter of serious music, Musica Viva Australia, presents thousands of concerts each year across Australia. Sydney holds free — and hugely popular — open-air opera and classical concerts each year in the Domain as part of the Sydney Festival.

Jazz clubs exist in all the big cities, where you might hear a visiting celebrity or an up-and-coming local band. Plenty of pubs feature jazz, but usually on weekends only. Both indoor and outdoor jazz concerts are also advertised.

Other music — folk, pop, rock or rap — can reveal something of a nation's soul. Aussie options range from a bearded troubadour dishing out bush ballads in an Outback saloon to hard-hitting metal bands. Contemporary groups such as Silverchair, Powderfinger, and Savage Garden follow in the wake of past notables like the Seekers, the Bee Gees, Men at Work, INXS, Midnight Oil, AC/DC, and Cold Chisel.

Nightlife depends on the size of the town. You won't find Jennifer Lopez or Sir Elton John performing in Burrumbuttock, New South Wales, but nightlife in Australia's smaller towns and remoter areas can still be a load of fun, as anyone who has attended an Outback bush dance or seen that wacky Australian movie *The Adventures of Priscilla, Queen of the Desert* will know.

In larger centers and cities, nightlife venues, acts, and attractions are listed in guides published in daily newspapers, usually on Thursdays or Fridays. Posters slapped on walls and telegraph poles proclaim dance parties, gigs, plays, and concerts. Musical pubs and private clubs provide more mainstream entertainment; it's usually quite easy for non-members to enter the latter. Clubs subsidize their meals and entertainment with profits from their slot machines, called poker machines (more affectionately, pokies). For punters who prefer to wager serious money, gambling **casinos** are available in big cities and resorts. Usually open very late into the night, casinos are typically equipped for, among other pursuits: roulette, craps, keno, blackjack, baccarat, and the backwoods game of two-up (see page 135) in a more refined, electronic version.

Cinema. Nicole Kidman is probably Australia's best-known contemporary film star. Others include Judy Davis, Geoffrey Rush (winner of the 1997 best actor Oscar for *Shine*), and the great swashbuckler, Errol Flynn, who hailed from Tasmania. New Zealand-born Russell Crowe — who won the 2001 best actor Oscar for *Gladiator* — lives in Australia while not making movies, and Mel Gibson grew up in Australia.

Founded at the end of the 19th century, the Australian film industry took a great leap forward in the 1970s and has never really looked back. Films such as *Picnic at Hanging Rock, My Brilliant Career, Breaker Morant,* the *Mad Max* series, and *Crocodile Dundee* — as well as the more off-beat *Strictly Ballroom,* and *The Adventures of*

Priscilla, Queen of the Desert — have given audiences around the world a glimpse of Australia's scenery and perhaps provided insight into the national character and preoccupations. *The Piano* and *Muriel's Wedding* also excelled. Multi-screen cinema complexes are popular in town centers as well as suburbs. Big cities also have specialized cinemas showing art films, foreign films, and revivals.

SHOPPING

In most cities, the browsers and window-shoppers congregate along the pedestrian malls. Department-store chains such as David Jones, Grace Bros, and Myer provide a dependable cross-section of what's available. Downtown arcades and courts are crammed with smaller boutiques handling everything from high fashion to silly souvenirs.

In Sydney the skyscrapers have subterranean shopping arcades; the QVB by Town Hall station is a great place to browse. In Melbourne the main shopping streets are Collins and Bourke, and the Bourke Street Mall. Rundle Street Mall is the essence of shopping in Adelaide, and traffic-free Hay Street Mall is Perth's sprawling equivalent.

Shopping hours usually run nonstop from 8:30am or 9am to 5pm or 5:30pm, Monday to Friday, and until 5pm on Saturdays in major towns and cities. One night a week, either Thursday or Friday depending on the city, the stores stay open until about 9pm. In larger cities, tourist needs are catered to on Sundays as well. Some big-city stores operate 24 hours a day.

What To Buy

Here's a brief survey of the distinctive shopping possibilities to keep in mind as you travel across Australia.

Aboriginal arts and crafts. Some good places to come across authentic boomerangs, didjeridoos (drone pipes), and works of art are the Northern Territory and North Queensland, but you can find Aboriginal products in specialty stores all over the country. Outback artists produce traditional paintings on bark, the subjects and style recalling the prehistoric rock paintings featuring kangaroos, emus, fish, snakes, crocodiles, and impressions of tribal ceremonies. Other indigenous painters use modern materials to produce canvases in a style that looks uncannily like some abstract-expressionist work, yet recounting Dreamtime legends and rituals. If the themes are old, the economics are contemporary; the price tags on paintings may go into four or even five figures.

Fine workmanship is also seen on some of the painted wood sculptures of animals and birds. You'll see large, brightly decorated didjeridoos — indigenous wind instruments made from tree trunks hollowed out by obliging termites. Slightly easier to transport are clap-sticks for percussion accompaniment. Some Aboriginal craftsmen also produce decorated wooden shields and, somewhat inevitably, boomerangs.

A word of warning: fakes and kitsch are sometimes represented as Aboriginal art by unscrupulous traders. To help identify genuine Aboriginal and Torres Strait Islander art, cultural products, and services, Aboriginal communities have developed the Label of Authenticity, which uses the Aboriginal colors black, red, and yellow and is protected by law.

Antiques include some worthy colonial pieces: furniture, clocks, jewelry, porcelain, silverware, glassware, and maps. Some dealers specialize in non-Australian antiques, for instance Chinese ceramics or Japanese screens. In Sydney, the Paddington district is full of antiques shops. Melbourne's antiques center is High Street, Armadale.

Diamonds are mined by Argyle Diamond Mines in the rugged Kimberley region in the country's west; Australia is one of the world's largest diamond sources. Kimberley is famed for its "pink" diamonds, sometimes marketed under the description "champagne." Hues range from lightly flushed to deep red.

Duty-free shopping is highly organized throughout Australia, not just at airports but also in the cities. Regulations require the

A display of ceramic sculptures at Apollo Bay, Victoria, a gem of natural beauty and a center for the arts.

duty-free chains to offer goods at their airport shops at the same price as their downtown outlets. You will be required to produce your air ticket and passport at the duty-free store; you mustn't open the packages before you leave the country; on your departure you are obliged to show them to the customs agent, who'll be looking for you.

Fashions. The season just ending in Australia is always about to begin north of the equator — so Australian end-of-season sales can deliver bargains that are instantly wearable when you return home. "Wearable art" in swimwear, fashion garments, fabrics, and souvenirs proliferates. Names to look for include Ken Done, Desert Designs, Balarinji Australia, Country Road, Covers, Trent Nathan, Lizzie Collins, Studibaker Hawk, Perri Cutten, Von Troska, Alannah

Hill, Jodie Boffa, Scanlan & Theodore, Morissey Edmiston, Collette Dinnigan, Saba, and Robert Burton.

Kangaroo-skin souvenirs include toy kangaroos and koalas and other such products — some of them are quite trite. The cheapest of the stuffed kangaroos and koalas, often wrapped up in patriotic Australian packaging, are imported. One widespread and distinctly Aussie item is the kangaroo-scrotum purse — a must for the collector of bad-taste souvenirs!

Opals

Australia is the source of about 95 percent of the world's opals. "White" opals are mined from the fields of Andamooka and Coober Pedy in South Australia, where inhabitants live underground to escape searing summer heat. "Boulder" opals — bright and vibrant — come from Quilpie in Queensland while the precious "black" opal (actually more blue than black) is mined at Lightning Ridge and White Cliffs in New South Wales. Opals, considered among Australia's best buys, are sold unset or as finished jewelry. Larger jewelry shops can arrange duty-free purchase for foreign visitors, but you may have to pay duty when you arrive home. The products are virtually unmatched.

Shimmering Australian South Sea pearls are prized worldwide.

Outback clothing

A distinct style of clothing has evolved from rural Australia, an area collectively known as "The Bush." Driza-bone oilskin raincoats, Akubra hats (wide-brimmed hats usually made of felt), and the R. M. Williams range of bush wear (including boots and moleskin trousers) are good examples. Consider a pair of Blundstone boots, made in Tasmania and renowned for their durability.

Paintings and prints by contemporary Australian artists are on show in commercial galleries in many areas, but the biggest concentration is in the big cities. Sydney galleries are clustered in the central shopping district and in Paddington. In Melbourne visit the City, Toorak Road, and High Street, Armadale. They'll handle the packing, insurance, and shipping details for you.

Sapphires. After opals, sapphires are Australia's most-mined gemstones. A sapphire is exactly the same stone as a ruby — the only difference is the name and the color. Creative Australian jewelers work wonders with sapphires.

Sheepskin. If it isn't too hot to think about it, Australia offers a wide range of sheepskin boots, hats, coats, rugs, and novelty items.

Souvenirs, ingenious or hackneyed, indigenous or imported, pop up everywhere you travel: in cities, resorts, and along the way at roadside stands. Tourists seem unable to resist miniature kangaroos, koalas and, in Tasmania, almost-lovable Tasmanian devil dolls. A selection of plastic boomerangs and beer can-holders head the very long list of less artistic souvenirs, followed by saucy T-shirts. In Sydney, you'll find them cheap at Paddy's Market. In Melbourne, try Queen Victoria Market.

Woolen goods. It's those sheep again: Look for high-quality sweaters and scarves, and tapestries, too. You can also buy hand-spun wool. Australian merino sheep produce fine fleece ideally suited for spinning. All kinds of knitwear, from vivid children's clothing to Jumbuk brand greasy wool sweaters (which retain their natural water resistance), are available.

Champions Galore

Australia has produced so many sporting heroes that no hall of fame could hold them all. Here's a rundown of some of the internationally celebrated names of modern times.

Cricket

- Don Bradman
- Greg Chappell
- Dennis Lillee
- Rodney Marsh
- Merv Hughes
- Mark Waugh

Swimming

- John Marshall
- Dawn Fraser
- Samantha Riley
- Kieren Perkins
- Grant Hackett
- Ian Thorpe
- Shane Gould

Golf

- Jim Ferrier
- Peter Thompson
- David Graham
- Greg Norman
- Robert Allenby

Track Events

- John Landy
- Herb Elliot
- Ron Clarke
- Cathy Freeman

Tennis

- Frank Sedgman
- Ken Rosewall
- Lew Hoad
- Rod Laver
- Roy Emerson
- Evonne Goolagong
- Margaret Court
- Pat Cash
- Mark Philippousis

FESTIVITIES

Not many tourists would plan their whole trip to coincide with the begonia festival in Ballarat, the Bendigo bonsai exhibition, or even the crazy dry-river regatta in Alice Springs. But knowing when and where the special events are scheduled might add that extra splash of local color to your holiday.

January

- Sydney Festival, a month of concerts, drama, exhibitions, sports, and special events.

- Perth Cup horseracing classic takes place at Royal Ascot Racecourse.

- Country Music Festival, Tamworth.

- Australian Tennis Open.

- Hobart Summer Festival, a six-week-long celebration of arts, culture, and food.

- Port Lincoln Tunarama Free Festival on the foreshore of Boston Bay, with world tuna-throwing championships.

- First Wine in the World Celebration at the Chateau Hornsby Winery, Alice Springs. On 1 January, just after midnight, watch as the shiraz grapes are made into the the 'early red,' the first wine anywhere in the world in any given year.

February

- Perth Festival, sporting and cultural events.

- Adelaide Festival of Arts (even-numbered years), three weeks of opera, ballet, theater, art, and literary events.

- Womadelaide, world music festival (odd-numbered years) in Adelaide.

- Launceston Cup, the social event of Tasmania. Much more than just a horse race, it is the culmination of a one month racing calendar.

March and April

- Sydney Gay and Lesbian Mardi Gras Parade, fun-filled, provocative parade along Oxford Street.

- Australian Formula 1 Grand Prix.

- Moomba Festival, Melbourne swings with fireworks, music, river pageants, and a street parade.

- Australian Grand Prix, Albert Park, Melbourne, the first round of the Formula 1 World Championship.

- Canberra National Multicultural Festival.

- Barossa Valley, South Australia Vintage Festival, celebrating the wine harvest (odd-numbered years) with German-Australian gaiety.

- Sydney Royal Easter Show, near Olympic Park.

- Sydney Cup Week, a pageant of horseracing.

May

- Barossa Valley Balloon Regatta, held Nuriootpa in the Barossa Valley, this features dawn or late afternoon take-offs.

- Adelaide Cup horserace and associated festivities.

- Austalian Celtic Festival in New South Wales. This event is truly unique in that it is the only festival in Australia that does not discriminate between the various Celtic backgrounds and offers a uniting place for all people. Events include dancing, singing, street processions, open ceremony and stalls. The festival encourages and promotes Celtic music, knowledge, and history, ensuring a wonderful weekend, that encompasses all facets of Celtic fun.

June

•Darwin Beer Can Regatta, in which all the boats are ingeniously constructed of used beer cans.

•A Taste of Manly, Sydney's largest annual food and wine festival, this two-day event is a showcase for multicultural restaurants.

•Bounty Day Norfolk Island: On 8 June (anniversary of the Bounty mutineers' arrival in 1856 from Pitcairn Island), festivities culminate in a Bounty Ball.

•Brisbane Cup, horserace.

July

•Alice Springs Camel Cup, camel race.

•Gold Coast Marathon, Queensland.

•Melbourne Grand National Steeplechase.

•Royal Darwin Show, agricultural exhibition.

August and September

•Royal Queensland Show, Brisbane, agricultural roundup with animals, fireworks, and fun.

•Mt. Isa Rodeo and Festival, Queensland: Australia's biggest and most popular.

•Alice Springs Henley-on-Todd Regatta, bottomless boats racing hilariously on a waterless riverbed.

•Australian Masters Alpine Ski Races, Snowy Mountains.

•Royal Adelaide Show, South Australia's agricultural summit meeting.

- Royal Melbourne Show, 10 days of bucolic attractions, sports competitions, and amusements.

- Toowoomba Carnival of Flowers, Queensland, floral parade and gardening competitions.

- Various capital cities: Australian Rules football finals.

Birdsville Races, Outback Birdsville in Queensland (population 100) holds a weekend of races and revelry. An Australian classic! Floriade Canberra, the biggest display of flowers in Australia, complemented by music, dance, street theater, sculpture and food.

- Jabiru Wind Festival, the major annual cultural community event in the Alligator Rivers and Kakadu National Park region.

October

- Melbourne International Festival, international and local visual and performing arts.

- Australian Motorcycle Grand Prix.

- Royal Hobart Agricultural Show, Tasmania.

November

- The Melbourne Cup. One of the premier events on the world horseracing circuit, this renowned race brings Australia to a virtual standstill. A glorious celebration of horseflesh, champagne, and giant hats.

- Sydney Sleaze Ball, themed gay and lesbian party.

December

- Western Australian Turf Club Derby, horseraces.

- Sydney to Hobart Yacht Race.

- Various capital cities: New Year's Eve Celebrations with fireworks are gigantic, festive affairs.

EATING OUT

If you enjoy dining out at bargain prices, with a wide choice of menus reflecting varied ethnic influences, you're going to enjoy mealtimes in Australia's cities.

Eating well in the land down under doesn't carry an inflated price tag. The whole country boasts inexpensive bistros, cafés, and food markets where diverse and wholesome cuisine can be savored at moderate prices. Current exchange rates with major world currencies make Australia even more of a gastronomic bargain.

All state capitals have a lively café scene and most support "BYO." Those initials stand for "bring your own" and allow you to take along store-bought wine to enjoy with your meal. Australian wine is relatively inexpensive and of high-quality — you can buy it at pubs or from a wide variety of discount liquor outlets. Many other restaurants are licensed, with their own wine cellars.

The average urban-dwelling Australian eats out several times a week — a testimony to the quality and affordability of the food. In the words of Barbara Kafka, one of America's foremost food writers and cookbook authors, "Australians have one of the most extraordinary assortments of basic ingredients of high quality anywhere in the world, and at exceptionally modest prices."

On a visit in 1996, renowned chef and gourmet Robert Carrier went into raptures: "I've never had such tastes, such subtleties, such delights, such form, such color," he told *Australian Gourmet Traveller* magazine. At least half-a-dozen restaurateurs, if they set up in Paris, would be instant successes, Carrier declared.

Australian cooks have the advantage of using a wonderful palette of ingredients. The country's climatic diversity provides a wide range of fresh vegetables and fruits, ranging from exotic rambutans, coconuts, and lychees to apples and spinach.

This culinary wonderland is relatively new. During most of the two centuries of modern Australia's existence, its inhabitants subsisted on bland "meat and veg" fodder. Cultural intermingling since World War II has revolutionized the national diet. Urban Australia now eats what has been described as "fusion food" — a collage of culinary influences that enlivens basic fish, grain, or meat with, for example, a handful of chopped coriander, a splash of olive oil, and a dash of chili.

If you're into exotic fare, sample goat cheeses from Western Australia, cold-pressed olive oils from South Australia, buffalo-milk mozzarella from New South Wales, or oysters, salmon, and other seafood ingredients from Tasmania.

The gastronomic revolution has yet to take hold in most working-class suburbs, or in rural areas. A typical menu in a small-

Adelaide has an abundance of cafés and restaurants — something to suit every taste.

Indigenous Dining

Innovations by Australian chefs since 1990 have included the increasing use of indigenous foods in fine dining. Lemon aspen, bush tomatoes, Illawarra plums, lemon myrtle, lilli pillies, muntari berries, and other mysterious ingredients have begun to appear on restaurant menus, often blended with traditional dishes of meat and fish. Kangaroo and emu are commercially farmed and processed. Both meats are low in fat content and high in fiber.

Collectively known as native food — or sometimes, bush tucker — these are just some of the fruits, seeds, nuts, fungi, mammals, reptiles, fish, and birds that sustained Australia's indigenous inhabitants for up to 100,000 years before white settlers came to the region.

Other bush-tucker ingredients include quandongs (like a peach with a touch of rhubarb), wattle seeds (sometimes used in ice cream), Kakadu plums (less sweet than the usual variety), and bunya bunya nuts (delicious in satay sauces). Bunya bunya nuts are a little like macadamias — which, incidentally, are also native to Australia and were introduced to Hawaii from Queensland in the 19th century.

Even wilder Aboriginal ingredients, not yet widespread in restaurants, include the Bogong moth (a hefty moth roasted in a fire and eaten like a peanut) and the witchetty grub (a puffy, white grub found in the trunks and roots of certain wattle trees). The witchetty grub has been shown to be a virtual powerhouse of protein, fat, and energy. Don't worry too much about the fat — most of the fatty acids are mono-unsaturated. Cooking tip: It's best to cook the grubs quickly in the ashes of a fire until they swell and the skin stiffens.

Harborside restaurants are a pleasant place to pass an evening under the Australian sky.

town café will probably include nothing more exotic than moussaka or spaghetti Bolognese. The traditional Aussie meat pie, doused liberally with tomato sauce, rules supreme in these outposts, as does the hamburger. Outside the standardized US chains, Australian hamburgers tend to include beetroot and lettuce rather than pickle.

What to Eat

Breakfast is anything you want it to be, from muesli and grapes or coffee and croissant to steak and eggs. Depends where you are and your hunger level.

Fish and seafood. Fish adorning the Australian menu include the delicious snapper, the meaty John Dory, smallish flounder, and bigger sole, the bony but flavorsome whiting (no relation to the English whiting), and the tropical trevally. Then there's barramundi, which means "big scales" in an Aboriginal language, and is found in both fresh and salt water; game fishermen in the north take "barra" of up to 15 kg (33 lbs). Along the Barrier Reef they even eat red emperor, a fish so gorgeous it might take a snorkeler's breath away.

Treat yourself to succulent seafood specialties such as Sydney rock oysters, as delicious as any in the world, and Brisbane's famous Moreton Bay bug, a crustacean to gloat over, and gloriously meaty mud crabs. Lobster, grilled or thermidor, is for special occasions. You are also likely to come across some of the lobster's freshwater cousins, known locally as yabbies. Prices are

Grapevines dot the landscape in Barossa, South Australia where winemaking is a fine art.

Wine casks line the walls of a wine cellar in the Barossa Valley, the country's best known wine region.

less forbidding when it comes to steamed mussels or prawns (shrimps). A popular and simple Australian *al fresco* meal for two consists of a kilo (2.2 pounds) of prawns and a bottle of ice-cold white wine. Scrumptious!

Meat favorites include beefsteak or roast lamb. You can even dine on kangaroo or emu if you're feeling adventurous. The BSE ("mad cow disease") problem affecting European beef does not affect Australia. Meat pies are a long-established staple.

Vegetables are available in as much variety as anywhere else in the world, but some restaurants prefer to serve meat dishes with salad — mainly because it doesn't require cooking and is easier to prepare. If you want vegetables, ask for them. Many Australian chefs are willing to accommodate customer requests.

Georgian habits

Mercifully for public health and safety, the wild rum-drinking of the young Australian colony has abated. Aussies have switched tastes to beer or wine. Statistics released for the year 1997 showed that Australians had slipped to fifth in the world beer consumption league at 93.26 liters (197 US pints) a head, a drop of 5.83 liters (12.3 US pints) since 1993. Ahead of Australia (in order) were the Czech Republic, Germany, Belgium, and Great Britain. Following Australia came the US, the Netherlands, Spain, Hungary, and Colombia.

Even so, Australians drink almost four times more beer than the world average. A health report released in 1999 revealed that the average Australian 12-year-old boy downs 3.5 alcoholic drinks a week and the average girl of the same age drinks 2.3 alcoholic drinks a week.

Prolific Australian author Thomas Keneally, writer of Schindler's Ark (basis of Steven Spielberg's movie Schindler's List), contends that Australians have remained essentially Georgian in character. Keneally draws parallels between Georgian England and the contemporary Australian ethos, which include: "a frenzy for gaming and gambling," a combination of rebelliousness and conservatism — and a deep respect for heavy alcoholic consumption.

Fruit in Australia covers all the climatic zones. To name a few: the more familiar apples, cherries, plums, and berries from the temperate latitudes; and tropical avocados, bananas, papayas, passion fruit, pineapples, and mangoes.

Desserts. You'll be able to find as many as you might want. A traditional Australian favorite is the light and fluffy *pavlova*, a meringue concoction traditionally topped with kiwi fruit. It's a little unfashionable these days, but worth sampling if you can get it.

Australian Wines

Australian wines are among the world's best — a judgment confirmed consistently at international wine shows. Wine is one of Australia's most important export industries and the range sold in liquor stores is extensive and moderately priced.

Australia's interest in wine production stretches back a couple of centuries. The founder of the New South Wales colony, Captain Arthur Phillip, had his priorities right. One of the first projects he ordered in 1788 was the planting of vines at Sydney Cove. Because of factors like the damp and the sea breezes, the site (now part of Sydney's Botanic Gardens) was quite wrong for growing grapes, which developed "black spot," and the experiment failed. But in 1791 three acres of vines were successfully planted a few miles inland.

Rum, rather than wine, became the favorite drink under Governor Phillip's successor. Free-enterprising army officers enjoyed a monopoly on the staggeringly profitable sales of rum, and widespread abuses were reported to London. It was Captain William Bligh, the original hardliner of *Bounty* fame, who was dispatched to clean up Australia. Governor Bligh was deposed in the Rum Rebellion of 1808, a mutiny led by one of the first wine-growers, John Macarthur.

Today, most Aussie wine varieties are identical to those sold in the US or Europe. Note, however, that the red wine varietal marketed in America as sirrah or syrah is called shiraz in Australia (the first of which is made just after midnight on 1 January; see page 202).

Australian wines have become so popular in Britain that they have eclipsed wines from Spain, Germany, and Italy to become second only to French wines in sales.

Wine is produced in every Australian state, even cool Tasmania and the baking hot Northern Territory (where a small "chateau" holds forth on the edge of Alice Springs). The biggest producer is South Australia, where the best-known wineries are situated in the beautiful Barossa Valley. The most important wine-producing region of New South Wales is the Hunter Valley. Victoria boasts numerous wine-growing regions, and Western Australia's Swan Valley and Margaret River areas have also made their mark.

If you're interested in seeing where the wine comes from, every state capital has wine-growing areas nearby, and the chance to sample wines at the cellar door is one of their best features. As most wineries are concentrated in a relatively small area, they make ideal touring for a day or — better still — two days, either independently or on a guided tour.

The Amber Nectar

Beer in Australia is served very cold. Australia's best-known beer is probably Fosters lager, but that's only one of many varieties that exist. Reschs, Tooheys, Victoria Bitter, XXXX (a brand from Queensland), Swan, and Cascade are popular brands. Some beers are sold in "new" and "old" types, the first being lager and the latter darker in color. Coopers beer from South Australia is a favorite among connoisseurs — it's rich and strong, similar to the best British real ales.

Australia's standard alcoholic strength for canned beer is 4.9 per cent — pretty strong by international standards. A word of advice for weight-watchers from America: The word "light" or "lite" applied to beer in Australia means lighter in alcohol, not lighter in calories. It has exactly the same calorific content as the regular type. The alcoholic strength of Australian beer must by law be displayed on the can or bottle.

HANDY TRAVEL TIPS

An A–Z Summary of Practical Information

A

ACCOMMODATIONS (see also CAMPING, YOUTH HOSTELS)
Australia welcomes the traveler with all kinds of accommodations. The luxury end of the spectrum matches the most sumptuous world standards, in the rooms and suites as well as the associated restaurants, lounges, saunas, and spas. But even in budget-priced hotel and motel rooms you can expect a private shower or bath and toilet, a telephone, a TV set, a small refrigerator, and coffee and tea-making equipment (and free coffee, tea, and milk). In most areas air-conditioning, or at least a ceiling fan, is provided.

There's no limit to the level of luxury a hotel or motel can attain, and either type can be anywhere — along the highway or right downtown. Distinguishing between the two can be confusing. The only sure difference is that a hotel has a bar open to the public — indeed, the most modest ones have little else to offer. Adding to the confusion: "hotel" is also a synonym for "pub" here. If a motel has a bar, it's usually strictly for the guests. You can't judge a hostelry by what it calls itself.

Private hotels, often small guesthouses, do not have a license for alcohol. Bed-and-breakfast establishments — private homes taking paying guests — exist in towns or out on the farms. Big towns and resorts also have self-catering apartments with maid service and fully-equipped kitchens, convenient for longer stays.

Overseas offices of the Australian Tourist Commission <www.australia.com> have listings of hotels and motels. You can reserve accommodations through your travel agent, the nearest offices of the international and Australian hotel chains, or your airline. Within Australia, the state tourist bureaus, domestic airlines, and hotel chains offer instant, free bookings. If you arrive out of the blue, local tourist offices have desks for last-minute reservations.

Accommodations may be hard to find when Australians themselves go traveling by the million, during school holidays. These can vary, but most states have adopted a four-term school year with two-week breaks in April, June/July, and September/October. The Christmas/summer holidays are from mid-December to the beginning of February.

AIRPORTS

The principal gateways are Melbourne, Sydney, Brisbane, Darwin, and Perth. Other international airports serve Adelaide, Townsville, Hobart, and Cairns. The domestic air network is very well-developed, and even smallish towns usually have comfortable, efficient terminals. The biggest airports have the full range of restaurants and bars, newsstands, souvenir shops, post office, and banks. The international airports have duty-free shops for both arriving and departing passengers.

Arriving passengers can travel from airport to town by taxi or bus. In Sydney, Brisbane, Adelaide, Darwin, and Perth, airport bus service goes to and from the door of most hotels. Travel time ranges from 20 minutes (Perth and Darwin) to 40 minutes (Sydney). Note that Sydney Airport's domestic and international terminals are a shuttle-bus ride apart. A rail link between Sydney Airport and Sydney Central Station opened in 2000.

Check-in time for departing passengers on domestic flights is 30 minutes before the scheduled flight time; international flights require check-in at least 90 minutes in advance.

B

BICYCLE RENTAL

Most Australian cities are reasonably attuned to cyclists and bicycle lanes are sometimes marked on inner-city streets. Cars clog large cities, however, and attempts to cater to cyclists are often little more than cosmetic. Canberra is an exception; cycling there is excellent.

Australia

Organized cycle tours of varying lengths are available, including transportation to and from a scenic area (bikes provided), food, and accommodations. You can also rent touring bikes. For details, look up "Bicycles & Accessories — Retail & Repairs" in the Yellow Pages phone book of the relevant city. Local cycling organizations are a good source of information:

Bicycle Federation of Australia, Tel. (03) 9827 4453 <www.bfa.asn.au>.

Pedal Power ACT (Canberra), Tel. (02) 6248 7995 <www.sunsite.anu.edu.au.community/pedalpower>.

Bicycle New South Wales, Tel. (02) 9283 5200 <www.bicyclensw.org.au>.

Bicycle Queensland, Tel. (07) 3844 1144 <www.uq.net.au/~zzbikeq>.

Bicycle Institute of South Australia, Tel. (08) 8271 5824 <www.bisa.asn.au>.

Bicycle Victoria, Tel (03) 9328 3000 <www.bv.com.au>.

Throughout Australia, the law requires that cyclists wear helmets at all times.

BUDGETING FOR YOUR TRIP

You can eat out well for little money; a plate of noodles or pasta can cost A$8 or less. Exchange rates have shifted in favor of major foreign currencies in recent years, boosting the value even further.

Accommodations also represent good value when measured against equivalents in other developed countries. Air travel is a relatively high-ticket item, but the arrival of two new challengers on domestic air routes — Virgin Blue and Impulse Airlines — has triggered periodic spates of fare discounting. International passengers may be entitled to discounted travel within Australia, depending on the airline they arrived on and their fare type. International fares to Australia have fallen steadily in real terms over the past decade.

On the ground, train travel can be competitive for shorter distances, and budget long-distance coach operations abound.

Inflation in Australia has remained low for the past decade. In early 2001, the cost of a liter of petrol (gasoline) was approaching A$1.00, more expensive than in the US but cheaper than in most European countries.

C

CAMPING

Australians are avid campers, and you'll find campsites dotted all over the areas frequented by tourists. The sites tend to be jammed at school holiday times. They have at least the basic amenities, and in some cases much more in the way of comfort. Aside from roomy tents with lights and floors, some installations have caravans (trailers) or cabins for rent. Showers, toilets, laundry facilities, and barbecue grills are commonly available. The national parks generally have well-organized camping facilities; to camp beyond the designated zone you must ask the rangers for permission. There are coach tours for campers, or you can rent a campervan or motorhome by the day or week (see also CAR RENTAL).

CAR RENTAL

For seeing the Australian countryside at your own pace, there's no substitute for a car. Brisk competition among the international and local car rental companies means you can often find economical rates or special deals, for instance unlimited mileage or weekend discounts. Rates are considerably higher if you drive in remote country areas. In general, it's worth shopping around. But be careful — some cheap companies impose a metropolitan limit on vehicles. Check first, as your insurance won't be valid outside the designated area.

In busy locations you can rent anything from a super-economy model or a four-wheel-drive vehicle to a limousine with or without chauffeur. Campervans and caravans (trailers) are available, though most are reserved in advance for school holidays.

To rent a car you'll need a current Australian, overseas, or International Driver's License. The minimum age is 21, or in some cases 25. Third-party insurance is automatically included; for an additional fee you can also sign up for collision damage and personal accident insurance.

You can pick up a car in one city and return it elsewhere. Interstate arrangements are commonly available from the big firms like Avis <www.avis.com/au>, Hertz <www.hertz.com.au>, Thrifty <www.thrifty.com.au>, and Budget <www.budget.com.au>, which also have offices at airports. Campervans and caravans (trailers) are available, though many are reserved far in advance for school holiday periods.

CLIMATE

Travelers from the Northern Hemisphere find Australia's seasons upside down: Winter runs from June to August and Christmas comes in summertime. But it's much more complicated than that, for Australia covers so much ground, from the tropics to the temperate zone.

From November to March it's mostly hot, or at least quite warm, everywhere. In the north this period brings the rains, which can wash out roads and otherwise spoil vacation plans. In the south the nights, at least, are mild.

April to September is generally ideal in the tropics and central Australia — clear and warm. Occasional rain refreshes the south, with snow in the southern mountains.

By way of regional superlatives, Darwin is the state capital with the highest average hours of sunshine, but it also gets the most rain. Adelaide has the lowest average rainfall of all capital cities. Far to the south, Hobart is the coolest capital; its climate is similar to that of Britain. But statistics indicate that the cities of Australia bask in more sunshine than any others in the world.

For your guidance, here are the average daily maximum and minimum temperatures in degrees Fahrenheit:*

		J	F	M	A	M	J	J	A	S	O	N	D
Sydney	max.	79	77	77	72	66	63	61	63	68	72	75	77
	min.	64	64	63	59	52	48	46	48	52	55	59	63
Brisbane	max.	84	84	82	79	73	71	68	72	75	79	82	84
	min.	69	68	66	61	55	52	48	50	55	61	64	63
Alice	max.	99	97	91	84	73	68	66	72	79	88	93	95
Springs	min.	72	71	64	57	48	43	41	45	50	59	64	68
Perth	max.	86	86	82	75	71	64	63	64	66	71	77	81
	min.	64	64	63	57	54	50	48	48	50	52	57	61

And in degrees Celsius:

		J	F	M	A	M	J	J	A	S	O	N	D
Sydney	max.	26	25	25	22	19	17	16	17	20	22	24	25
	min.	18	18	17	15	11	9	8	9	11	13	15	17
Brisbane	max.	29	29	28	26	23	21	20	22	24	26	28	29
	min.	21	20	19	16	13	11	9	10	13	16	18	17
Alice	max.	37	36	33	29	23	20	19	22	26	31	34	35
Springs	min.	22	21	18	14	9	6	5	7	10	15	18	20
Perth	max.	30	30	28	24	21	18	17	18	19	21	25	27
	min.	18	18	17	14	12	10	9	9	10	11	14	16

* Minimum temperatures are measured just before sunrise, maximum temperatures in the afternoon.

CLOTHING

A sweater may come in handy, even in summer. After a hot day in the sun, the evening breeze can seem downright chilly. A light raincoat will serve in any season. Anywhere you go you'll need comfortable walking shoes. Because of the strong sun, a hat is advisable — particularly in the Outback.

While Sydneysiders dress casually on weekends (shorts, a short-sleeved shirt or T-shirt and sneakers or sandals are perfect), business attire can be surprisingly conservative. Visit any popular downtown pub in Sydney or Melbourne at lunchtime on a summer weekday and you encounter hundreds of men in dark blue suits and ties, trying to cope with the sweltering heat. Sydney has yet to adapt fully to its climate and adopt the open-necked informality seen in countries like Israel or the Philippines.

Restaurants have dropped the requirement for men to wear jacket and tie, but some establishments may refuse customers wearing T-shirts, tank tops, or ripped jeans. Entering clubs generally requires a collared shirt and covered shoes — no sneakers or sandals.

COMPLAINTS

If you think you've been overcharged or unfairly dealt with, the personal approach can be effective in plain-talking Australia. If not, consider contacting the travel agency that made the booking. Failing that, phone or write the Department of Fair Trading or Department of Consumer Affairs in the Australian state or territory concerned. Their contact details are listed in the phone book's White Pages, up front in the government section.

CRIME AND SAFETY

As in most countries, it's wise to take precautions against burglary and petty theft. Check your valuables in the hotel's safe deposit box. Lock your room and your car. Be alert for pickpockets in crowded buses and markets.

Overall, Australia is a safe place. Sydney's murder rate (two per each 100,000 citizens) is low by world standards and the city, Australia's biggest, has a relatively low crime rate. The same is true of other Australian cities, although muggings and fights are not unknown. It's best to avoid city parks after dark, particularly if on your own. Anti-drug laws vary greatly from state to state. Possession of small amounts of cannabis for personal use is generally either overlooked or dealt with by a fine. Narcotics are treated much more severely.

CUSTOMS AND ENTRY REQUIREMENTS

Australia is the only country in the western world to require all visitors to hold a visa. Citizens of New Zealand (which enjoys strong historical links with Australia) receive an automatic electronic visa when they present their passports at the Immigration counter.

Australia's Electronic Travel Authority (ETA), allows travel agents to issue an "invisible visa" electronically to visitors at time of booking in their home countries. Tourists or travelers visiting friends or relatives and wishing to stay for up to three months on each visit within a 12-month period should apply for the Tourist ETA (Type V), which is issued free. Those making a business visit should inquire whether they require a type BL or type BS visa.

The ETA eliminates having to find an embassy or consulate. The process can be completed in person or over the phone. This has greatly shortened the time most passengers have to wait at airport Customs and Immigration counters.

You can apply for a visa allowing multiple travel for up to four years, with a stay of three to six months on each visit. An application fee is then payable.

If you wish to extend your stay beyond three months, you will need to contact the nearest office of the Department of Immigration and Multicultural Affairs in Australia before the end of your three-month stay. ETAs are currently available to citizens of Andorra, Austria, Belgium, Brunei, Canada, Denmark, Finland, France, Germany, Greece, Iceland, Ireland, Italy, Japan, Liechtenstein, Luxembourg, Malaysia, Malta, Monaco, Netherlands, Norway, Singapore, South Korea, Spain, Sweden, Switzerland, UK, US, and Vatican City. The list is growing. The department's web sites <www.immi.gov.au> and <www.dima.gov.au> have the latest information.

Australia operates reciprocal working holiday programs with countries including Canada, Ireland, Japan, Korea, Malta, the

Netherlands, and the UK, for applicants between 18 and 25 (and in special circumstances, 26 to 30), either single or married without children. Working holiday visas allow recipients to work for up to three months at a time, over a one-year period.

You may have to show your return or onward ticket, and you may have to prove that you have sufficient funds for your stay.

On entry, you may take into Australia duty-free up to one liter of alcohol and 250 cigarettes or 250 grams of tobacco.

D

DRIVING

Road conditions: Australian roads are good considering the size of the country and the challenges of distance, terrain, and climate. Freeways link populous regions, but most country roads are two-lane highways which can be crowded at busy times.

Rules and Regulations: Like Britain, New Zealand, Japan, and many Asian countries, Australia drives on the left — which means the steering wheel is on the right and you overtake on the right. Drivers and passengers must wear seat belts. (The exception is buses, although many of them feature seat belts as an option). Car rental companies can supply suitable child restraints, boosters, and baby seats at an extra charge.

A tourist may drive in Australia on a valid overseas license for the same class of vehicle. Licenses must be carried when driving. If the license is in a language other than English, the visitor must carry a translation with the license. An International Driver's Permit is not sufficient by itself and must be accompanied by a valid driver's license.

The speed limit in cities and towns is generally 60 km/h (about 35 mph) but sometimes is cut to 40km/h (about 25 mph). Outside built-up areas the speed limit is generally either 100 km/h or 110 km/h (about 70 mph). There is no speed limit outside of built-up areas in the Northern Territory.

Throughout Australia, police make random checks for drugs or alcohol, using breath tests. The limit on alcohol in the blood is generally about 0.05, meaning in practice that three glasses of wine or three half-pint glasses of beer in an hour will take you to the limit. In NSW, if you are under 25 and in your first three years of driving, you must be under 0.02, which doesn't allow you to drink at all.

Outback driving: Check thoroughly the condition of your car and be sure you have a spare tire and plenty of spare drinking water. Find out about the fuel situation in advance and always be sure to leave word as to your destination and anticipated arrival time. Fill up the fuel tank at every opportunity, for the next station may be a few hundred kilometers away. Some dirt roads are so smooth you may be tempted to speed, but conditions can change abruptly. Be cautious with road trains, consisting of three or four huge trailers barreling down the highway towed by a high-powered truck. Pass them only with the greatest of care.

Parking: Heavy traffic and parking problems afflict some downtown areas. Parking meters and "no standing" zones are everywhere, so be careful.

If you need help: The Automobile Association <www.aaa.asn.au> is a national body that maintains links with similar organizations worldwide. Many state automobile associations have reciprocal arrangements with similar organizations overseas, so bring proof of your membership.

New South Wales: NRMA, 74-76 King Street, Sydney, NSW 2000; Tel. 132 132; <www.nrma.com.au>.

Victoria: RACV, 360 Bourke Street, Melbourne, Victoria 3000; Tel. 131 955; <www.racv.com.au>.

Queensland: RACQ, 300 St Pauls Terrace, Fortitude Valley, Queensland 4006; Tel. (07) 3361 2444; <www.racq.com.au>.

Australia

South Australia: RAA, 41 Hindmarsh Square, Adelaide, SA 5000; Tel. (08) 8202 4500; <www.raa.net>.

Tasmania: RACT, Corner of Patrick and Murray Streets, Hobart, Tasmania 7000; Tel. (03) 6232 6300; <www.ract.com.au>.

Western Australia: RACWA, 228 Adelaide Terrace, Perth, WA 6000; Tel. (08) 9421 4444; <www.rac.com.au>.

Northern Territory: AANT, 79-81 Smith Street, Darwin, NT 0800; Tel. (08) 8981 3837.

Fuel: Some filling stations are open only during normal shopping hours, so you may have to ask where after-hours service is available. Petrol (gasoline) in Australia comes in regular and premium grades, leaded and unleaded (all cars made in the past 10 years use unleaded) and is sold by the liter. In early 2001, it cost nearly A$1.00 a liter. Prices are often higher in country areas. Most stations are self-service and accept international credit cards.

Road signs: Signs are generally good, especially along heavily used roads. All distances are measured in kilometers. White-on-brown direction signs signal tourist attractions and natural wonders. To drive into the center of any city, simply follow the signs marked "City." Leaving a city is less straightforward: Exit routes are often signposted with the assumption that every driver has local experience, so you may require a good map and some advance planning. Most road signs are the standard international pictographs, but some are unique to Australia, such as large silhouette images of kangaroos or wombats, warning that you may encounter these animals crossing the road. Some signs use words, such as:

Crest steep	hilltop limiting visibility
Cyclist hazard	dangerous for cyclists
Dip	severe depression in road surface

Hump	bump or speed obstacle
Safety ramp	uphill escape lane from steep downhill road

E

ELECTRICITY

The standard throughout Australia is 230–250 volt, 50-cycle AC. Three-pronged plugs, in the shape of a bird's footprint, are universal. They are the same as in New Zealand and many Pacific countries. If from elsewhere, you will need an adapter. Many hotel rooms also have 110-volt outlets for razors and small appliances.

EMBASSIES/CONSULATES/HIGH COMMISSIONS

The embassies or high commissions of about 70 countries are established in Canberra, the national capital. They have consular sections dealing with passport renewal, visas, and other formalities. Some of them run major consular sections in Sydney, as well. To find the address of your consulate, look in the white pages of the telephone directory under "Consuls," or in the Yellow Pages under "Consulates and Legations".

Here are some major ones:

Embassy of the United States of America: Moonah Place, Yarralumla, ACT 2600; Tel. (02) 6214 5600.

High Commission of Canada: Commonwealth Avene, Yarralumla, ACT 2600; Tel. (02) 6270 4000

British High Commission (Consular Section): SAP House, Corner of Akuna and Bunda Streets, Canberra City, ACT 2601; Tel. (02) 6270 6666

New Zealand High Commission: Commonwealth Avenue, Canberra, Yarralumla, ACT 2600; Tel: (02) 6270 4211.

Embassy of Ireland: 20 Arkana Street, Yarralumla, ACT 2600; Tel. (02) 6273 3022.

Australia

South Africa High Commission: State Circle, Yarralumla, ACT 2600; Tel. (02) 6273 2424

EMERGENCIES
Ambulance — Fire — Police: Dial 000.
The 000 number — no coin required from public telephones — is in service in all cities and most towns. If you're in a remote area, however, look for the emergency numbers inside the front cover of the telephone directory. In the big cities there are round-the-clock dental emergency services as well as hospital emergency wards.

GAY AND LESBIAN TRAVELERS
Sydney's popular Gay and Lesbian Mardi Gras has helped make Sydney — and Australia — a popular destination for gay and lesbian travelers. Some tour operators, travel agents, and accommodations specialize in catering to a gay and lesbian clientele. Australian cities are generally tolerant towards gay and lesbian travelers but prejudice tends to increase in more remote, country areas. Homosexual acts are legal in all states. Sydney is one of the world's major gay cities, sometimes called "the gay capital of the Southern Hemisphere." Estimates of its gay population vary, but 400,000 is commonly quoted. Sydney's main gay precinct is Oxford Street (sometimes called "the Golden Mile") and the surrounding Darlinghurst area, with another precinct in King Street, Newtown.

GETTING TO AUSTRALIA
By Air. Flights from Asia, North America, and Europe serve international airports around Australia, of which Sydney's is by far the busiest. Sydney (and other Australian airports) are particularly busy around the Christmas holiday period, which coincides with midsummer. Fares are generally at their highest then,

and flights are heavily booked in both directions, so it's best to avoid midsummer travel if you are on a budget.

Australia is included in several "round-the-world" fare constructions — arrangements between two or more airlines which allow passengers to travel globally at bargain rates, provided they complete their journeys within a year and don't backtrack. Flight times to Sydney (approximate) are New York–Sydney 22 hours, Los Angeles–Sydney 15 hours, London–Sydney 21 hours. You can usually break the flight for a day or two at one of the stops along the way; in most cases this doesn't affect the price of the air ticket.

Flights from Asia, North America, and Europe go to Sydney, Cairns, or Melbourne, but you can also fly directly to Darwin, Perth, Brisbane, or Adelaide from many international points.

By Sea. No passenger liners operate to or from Australia anymore, but some Australian ports, notably Sydney and Cairns, feature in the itineraries of cruise ships. You can fly to locales like Bali or Singapore and embark on the cruise liner there, sail to Australia, then fly home from any Australian city, or resume the cruise at another port. It tends to be an involved process, however. Travel agents have cruise line schedules and brochures.

GUIDES AND TOURS

Tour companies offer a broad choice of excursions, from a day-trip to Canberra to long-haul journeys into the Outback. There are also local walking tours and tours for cyclists, wildlife-lovers and others catering to special interests.

H

HEALTH AND MEDICAL CARE

Standards of hygiene are high, particularly in food preparation. Doctors and dentists are proficient and hospitals well-equipped. If you fall ill, your hotel can call a doctor or refer you to one, or you can ask your embassy, high commission, or consulate for a list of approved doctors.

You should take out health insurance before departure to cover your stay in Australia. Also ensure that you have personal insurance or travel insurance with a comprehensive health component to cover the possibility of illness or accident.

Medicare, Australia's national health insurance, covers visitors from New Zealand, the UK, Ireland, Malta, Sweden, Italy, Finland, and the Netherlands. To be eligible, contact your national health program before traveling to Australia to ensure that you have the correct documents to enroll at any Medicare office on arrival in Australia. The agreement provides urgent treatment but doesn't cover elective surgery, dental care, ambulance services, or illness arising en route to Australia. The agreements do not cover repatriation in the case of illness or injury.

You are allowed to bring "reasonable quantities" of prescribed, non-narcotic medications. All should be clearly labeled and identifiable. For large quantities, bring a doctor's certificate to produce to Customs if necessary. All medication must be carried in personal hand luggage. Local pharmacies, called chemists, can fill most prescriptions — which must be written by an Australian-registered doctor.

Health hazards exist on the seas and in the countryside, starting with the threat of too much sun. High-factor sun-screen cream is essential if exposed, even on cloudy days.

Poisonous spiders live in Australia. The Sydney funnelweb, dark and bulbous, is one of the world's most lethal and aggressive. Although its bites are rare (about 10 victims a year), they require immediate medical attention to stave off coma and death. Catch the spider for identification if you can. Other poisonous spiders include the redback, the eastern mouse spider, and the white-tail.

Shark attacks are rare also, but one is too many and may well be your last. In 2000, sharks killed more people in Australia than anywhere else. (Before you get too alarmed, the death toll was three — out of seven attacks in Australian waters.) Swim between the flags and heed shark alarms.

In certain seasons and areas, bluebottles and other dangerous jellyfish may be encountered. Their sting is agonizing but can be treated. In the north of Australia, crocodiles can be a menace to swimmers. Obey the signs. Other marine hazards include the camouflaged stonefish and the blue-ringed octopus. Both can cause convulsions, paralysis, and death. Several of the world's deadliest snakes, including the brown snake, tiger snake, taipan, and death adder, live in Australia. You are unlikely to encounter them in built-up areas. The inland taipan, or fierce snake, has the most potent venom in the world, but is restricted to sparsely populated areas of southwest Queensland, so few people are bitten. If bitten by any snake, seek immediate medical attention.

The good news is that you can drink water from taps (faucets) anywhere unless specifically marked otherwise. In the Outback, warnings may read "Bore water" or "Not for drinking."

HITCHHIKING

It's better not to hitchhike, which is banned on freeways and throughout the whole state of Queensland. Even where it is tolerated, it can be risky. Some city hostels feature notice boards where people driving interstate can advertise for a traveling companion to share costs. That way, you at least get to meet the person you might travel with. Cut-rate bus travel is a safer and better option.

HOLIDAYS

1 January	New Year's Day
26 January	Australia Day
25 April	Anzac Day
25 December	Christmas Day

Australia

26 December	Boxing Day
Moveable dates:	Good Friday, Easter, Easter Monday, Queen's Birthday

Certain other public holidays are celebrated only in certain states, while other holidays are observed at different times in different states. School holidays arrive four times a year; the longest one is in the summer through the latter part of December and all of January, tending to crowd hotels and tourist attractions.

L

LANGUAGE

Australian is spoken everywhere. The vernacular is sometimes called Strine, which is the way the word "Australian" sounds in an extreme Australian pronunciation. While educated and cultivated Australians tend to speak in more neutral accents, Strine in the backblocks can sound to an American or European ear like a profound Cockney intonation piped through the nose. Foreigners who listen carefully usually understand what's said, at least when it's repeated.

Here are a few Australian terms and colloquialisms:

back of beyond	the Outback
billabong	water hole
bush	country area
bushranger	outlaw
dinkum	authentic
dinky-di	the truth
footy	rugby football
fossick	to search for precious stones
joey	baby kangaroo
Kiwi	New Zealander
mate	friend
ocker	Australian

Oz	Australia
paddock	field; fenced
Pom, Pommy	English person
ripper	exciting
roo	kangaroo
root	sex
station	ranch
tinny, or tube	can of beer
tucker	food
ute	utility truck
whinge	to complain

LAUNDRY AND DRY CLEANING

Hotels and motels usually offer one-day laundry and dry cleaning service for guests, but it can be quite expensive. Ask the receptionist, porter, or maid. Many hotels and motels also have laundromat facilities on the premises.

M

MAPS

State and local tourist offices give away useful maps of their areas. If you are in need of more detailed maps, check at newsstands and bookstores. Car rental companies often supply free city directories showing each street and place of interest. If driving beyond the cities you'll want to buy an up-to-date road map of the region.

MEDIA

More than 500 newspapers are published in Australia, ranging from internationally esteemed big city dailies like the *Sydney Morning Herald* and *The Age* of Melbourne to numerous backwoods weeklies. Among the latter are local periodicals aimed at the various immigrant communities, written in Dutch, French, German, Greek, Italian, and other languages.

Australia

In the bigger cities, specialist newsstands provide airmail copies of newspapers from London, Rome, New York, and Paris, in addition to weekly and monthly American and European magazines.

CNN and other satellite news services are available at most international-standard hotels — or you may be able to read your hometown paper on the Internet at one of the many Internet cafés around Australia.

MONEY

You don't have to reach for a credit card to use plastic in Australia — banknotes are made of it and feature transparent panels instead of watermarks. Australian currency is decimal, with the dollar the basic unit (100 cents equals one dollar). Notes come in $100, $50, $20, $10, and $5 denominations. Coins come in 5c, 10c, 20c, 50c, $1, and $2 denominations. As for credit cards, American Express, Bankcard, MasterCard, Visa, and Diners Club are widely accepted, but you may have problems with them in smaller towns and country areas and small retail shops.

All international airports in Australia provide currency exchange facilities, and foreign bills or travelers' checks can be converted at most banks. Cash travelers' checks at banks or larger hotels (despite the charges), as it may be difficult elsewhere. Know that Australian banks charge for just about everything these days.

ATM cards are widely used and machines are widespread. You may be able to obtain cash directly in this way using the same PIN number you use at home, provided your card has been validated for international access. EFTPOS is available at larger stores.

One quirk persists — it's still legal for shops to express prices in coins that no longer circulate. If something is priced at A$11.99, it will cost you $12.

OPEN HOURS

Banks. Generally open from 9:30am to 4pm Monday–Thursday and from 9:30am to 5pm on Fridays. In big cities, selected banking facilities may be available on Saturday morning, but don't bank on it. General office hours are 9am to 5pm, Monday–Friday, and post offices follow the same hours. Stamps are often available at the front desks of hotels and motels and at some retail outlets.

Shopping. Most shops close at 5pm or 5:30pm on weekdays. In most towns, shops have one (or sometimes two) late shopping nights a week, when stores stay open to 9pm or 9:30 pm. This is usually on Thursday or Friday. Sunday trading is becoming more common in larger cities, and some stores operate 24-hours a day.

Bars/pubs/hotels. Licensing hours vary by state, but a typical schedule would be 10am–10pm Monday–Saturday, with most pubs open by noon on Sundays as well.

POLICE

Each state operates its own police force, covering both urban and rural areas. The federal police force has jurisdiction over government property, including airports.

The police emergency telephone number is 000.

POST OFFICES

Australia's post offices are signposted "Australia Post." Most branches adhere to a 9am–5pm schedule Monday–Friday, though big-city General Post Offices often remain open for extended hours.

Postcards cost 95 cents to the US and $1 to Europe. Letters cost $1.05 and $1.20 respectively, and international aerograms cost 70 cents, whatever their destination. Mailboxes throughout Australia are red with an Australia Post logo. Most post offices have fax facilities, as do hotels. Internet cafés exist in all Australian cities and are spreading rapidly in small centers, too.

PUBLIC TRANSPORTATION

This is highly developed in most Australian cities, with buses and trains being the most frequent form. Sydney Airport is now connected directly to the city by rail.

Melbourne's trams (streetcars) are not only decorative — they're a vital part of city transportation. The gold-and-burgundy-colored City Circle tram is free. In Adelaide, trams run to Glenelg and the O-bahn provides highly efficient transportation. Sydney has its quirky monorail that links the central city and Darling Harbour, and also has a light rail system from Central Station to Chinatown, the Fish Markets, and beyond. A fine fleet of ferries, sailing from 6am–11pm daily, are concentrated at Circular Quay. The ferries provide cheap outings for sightseers to Kirribilli, Neutral Bay, or Taronga Zoo.

R

RELIGION

The major religion in Australia is Christianity. In the late 1990s, the numbers of Roman Catholics overtook the number of Anglicans (Church of England). Next in line (numbers-wise) are the Uniting Church, Presbyterian, and Orthodox. Of the non-Christian faiths, Muslims are the largest group, followed by Jews and Buddhists. To find the church of your choice, check at your hotel desk or look in the Yellow Pages of the telephone directory under "Churches and Synagogues." Most of the major religions will be represented.

T

TELEPHONE

Australia's country code is 61. This is followed by a city code, generally 2 for NSW or the ATC, 3 for Victoria and Tasmania, 7 for Queensland, and 8 for the Northern Territory, South Australia, or Western Australia.

Australia's telephone network is sophisticated; you can dial anywhere in the country from almost any phone, even in the Outback, and expect a loud and clear line. Many hotel rooms have phones from which you can dial cross-australia (STD) or internationally (IDD). Some hotels add a surcharge to your telephone bill.

The minimum cost of a local public payphone call is 40c. Long-distance calls within Australia (STD) and International Direct Dialing (IDD) calls can be made on Telstra public payphones. Check with the operator for these charges as they vary for distances and the time of day of the call. Public payphones accept most coins and Phonecards. A Phonecard is a pre-paid card for use in public payphones to make local, STD, and IDD calls. Phonecards are widely sold at newsstands and other shops, and come in denominations of $5, $10, $20 and $50. The Telstra PhoneAway pre-paid card enables you to use virtually any phone in Australia — home and office phones, mobile phones, hotel and payphones — all call costs are charged against the card. If you need assistance, help is available in seven languages.

Creditphones accept most major credit cards such as AMEX, Visa, and MasterCard and can be found at international and domestic airports, central-city locations and many hotels. Country Direct is a service that lets you speak directly with an operator in your home country or you can use an automated service. Cash is not needed as the call is charged to the receiving number or to your telephone credit card. Country Direct calling guides are available through Telstra shops, travel agents, and tour operators.

Phone books give full instructions on dialing and details on emergency and other services. To reach an overseas number, dial 0011, then the country code of the destination, the area code, and the local number.

TIME ZONES

Australia has three distinct time zones: Australian Eastern Standard Time (EST), which operates in New South Wales, Australian Capital Territory, Victoria, Tasmania, and Queensland; Central Standard Time (CST) in South Australia and Northern Territory (and in the NSW Outback city of Broken Hill); and Western Standard Time (WST) in Western Australia. CST is 30 minutes behind EST, while WST is two hours behind EST. Daylight saving (setting the clocks forward an hour) runs in New South Wales, the Australian Capital Territory (Canberra and surrounds), Victoria, and South Australia from the end of October through to the end of March, and in Tasmania from the beginning of October through to the end of March. The Northern Territory, Western Australia, and Queensland do not apply daylight saving during the summer.

Sydney is on EST, which is 10 hours ahead of Greenwich Mean Time and 15 hours ahead of New York. Time differences between Australia's zones and other countries vary seasonally as daylight saving is switched on and off by Australia or the other country. One way to get it right is to access <www.whitepages.com.au> on the Internet and use the time zone calculator.

TIPPING

Tipping is discretionary and a relatively recent custom. Nobody's livelihood depends on tipping. It is not customary to tip taxi drivers, porters at airports, or hairdressers, although you may do so if you wish. Porters have set charges at railway terminals, but not at hotels. Hotels and restaurants do not add service charges to accounts. In better-class restaurants, patrons sometimes tip food and drink waiters up to 10 percent, but only if service is good. (If you are ecstatic about the service, make it 15 percent!) Tipping is what it should be — an optional gratuity for good service. It has not developed into a means of subsidizing wages. If service is poor or a waiter is surly or impolite, don't tip.

TOILETS

Australians manage without euphemisms for "toilet," though in a country so rich in slang you won't be surprised to come across some wry synonyms. "Dunny" is the Outback slang term, but "washroom," "restrooms," "ladies," or "gents" are all understood. Toilets are often locked after certain hours, but you can generally use the facilities in any pub or cinema complex without needing to buy a drink or a movie ticket. Toilets are generally clean, even in the Outback. While on that subject, it's wise to check under Outback toilet seats to ensure no poisonous redback spider is lurking there. They like that location.

TOURIST INFORMATION

To obtain tourist information before you leave home, access the comprehensive web site of the Australian Tourist Commission (ATC) <www.austalia.com> or contact them in your country of residence or at their Australian head office: Level 4, 80 William Street, Woolloomooloo, Sydney, NSW 2011, Australia; Tel: 1300 361 650.

Overseas ATC offices are:

US: 2049 Century Park East, Suite 1920, Los Angeles CA, 90067, US; Tel (1-310) 229 4870; fax (1-310) 552 1215.

Korea: Suite 801, Hotel President 188-3, Ulchiro 1-ka, Chung-ku, Seoul 100-191 Korea; Tel (81-3) 5214 0720; fax (81-3) 5214 0719.

Australia

Hong Kong: Central Plaza, Suite 1501, 18 Harbour Road, Wanchai, Hong Kong; Tel (852) 2802 7700; fax (852) 2802 8211.

Taiwan: Trans-World Tourism Resources Inc, Suite 2208, 22nd Floor, World Trade Center, 333 Keelung Road, Section 1, Taipei, Taiwan; Tel (8862) 2757 7188; fax (8862) 2757 6483.

Singapore: #26-05 United Square, 101 Thomson Road, Singapore 307591, Republic of Singapore; Tel (65) 255 4555; fax (65) 253 8431.

United Kingdom: Gemini House, 10-18 Putney Hill, Putney, London SW15 6AA, UK; Tel (44-20) 8780 2229; fax (44-20) 8780 1496.

Japan: (Tokyo) c/o Australian Business Centre, New Otani Garden Court Building, 28F 4-1, Kioi-cho, Chiyoda-Ku Tokyo, 102 Japan. Tel (81-3) 5214 0720; fax (81-3) 5214 0719

Japan: (Osaka) OSCAT Building 4F (Osaka City Air Terminal) 1-4-1, Minata-machi Naniwa-ku, Osaka 556 Japan. Tel (81-6) 6635 3291; fax (81-6) 6635 3297.

New Zealand: Level 13, 44-48 Emily Place, Auckland 1, New Zealand. Tel (64-9) 379 9594; fax (64-9) 307 3117.

Once in Australia, even in the smallest town you will find an outlet distributing local tourist information and advice free of charge. Look for the international "I" sign.

W

WEBSITES

Australian Tourist Commission: <www.australia.com>

Travel Online: <www.travelonline.com>

Western Australian Tourism Commission:
<www.westernaustralia.net>

Northern Territory Tourist Commission: <www.nttc.com.au>

Tourism Tasmania: <www.tourism.tas.gov.au>

Tourism Victoria: <www.tourismvictoria.com.au>
Tourism New South Wales: <www.tourism.nsw.gov.au>
SouthAustralianTouristCommission: <www.southaustralia.com>
Tourism Queensland: <www.queensland-holidays.com.au>
Canberra Tourism: <www.canberratourism.com.au>
Visas: <www.immi.gov.au>
Latest currency exchange rates: <www.xe.net>
Australian Government: <www.fed.gov.au>
Sydney Morning Herald: <www.smh.com.au>
Melbourne Age: <www.theage.com.au>

WEIGHTS AND MEASURES

Since the 1960s, Australia has adhered to the metric system. Old-timers may still refer to distances in miles, and some inner-city, mock-Irish pubs persist in selling beer by the pint, but generally the abandonment of British Imperial measures has totally taken effect. See the following charts for some handy conversions.

Length

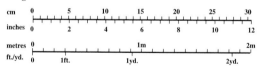

Weight

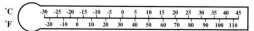

Temperature

°C
°F

Australia

Fluid measures

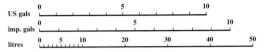

Distance

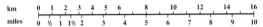

YOUTH HOSTELS

There are two types of hostel accommodations: privately-owned backpacker hostels and YHA Hostels (Youth Hostels Association). Both provide self-catering accommodations from about A$20 a night.

The Australian YHA is Australia's largest budget accommodations network, running more than 130 hostels in just about every place you might want to go in Australia. Youth is a comparative term, for the hostels are open to all ages and offer sleeping, self-catering kitchens and common rooms where you'll meet fellow travelers. You can join YHA in your own country or in Australia. Contact the YHA (422 Kent Street, Sydney, NSW 2001; Tel. (02) 9261 1111; <www.yha.com.au>) for a free information pack giving membership details and a list of hostels.

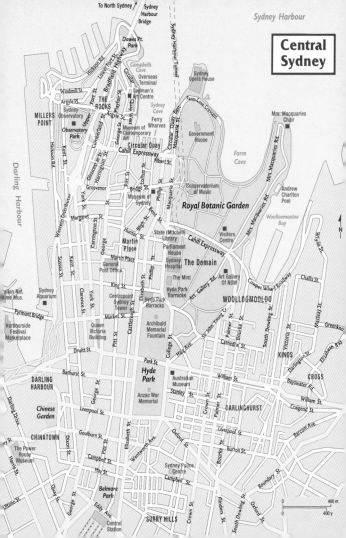

Central Sydney

Sydney Harbour

To North Sydney
Sydney Harbour Bridge
Sydney Harbour Tunnel

Dawes Pt. Park
Campbells Cove
Overseas Terminal
Cadman's Art Centre
Sydney Cove
Ferry Wharves
Museum of Contemporary Art
Sydney Opera House
Farm Cove Crescent
Government House
Mrs. Macquaries Chair

Windmill St.
Hickson Rd.
Bradfield Highway
Fort St.
Lower Fort St.
THE ROCKS
Sydney Observatory
Argyle Pl.
Argyle St.
Cumberland St.
George St.
Kent St.
Circular Quay
Farm Cove
Observatory Park
Upper Fort St.
Harrington St.

MILLERS POINT

Cahill Expressway
Albert St.
Conservatorium of Music
Andrew Charlton Pool
Woolloomooloo Bay

Hickson Rd.
Kent St.
Gloucester St.
Harrington St.
Grosvenor
Bridge St.
Museum of Sydney
Phillip St.
Macquarie St.
Royal Botanic Garden

Darling Harbour

Western Distributor
York St.
Carrington St.
George St.
Margaret
Hunter
Bligh St.
Pitt St.
State (Mitchell) Library
Parliament House
Sydney Hospital
Cahill Expressway
Visitors Centre
Mrs. Macquaries Rd.

Sussex St.
Kent St.
Clarence St.
George
Martin Place
General Post Office
Elizabeth St.
Castlereagh St.
King St.
Market St.
The Mint
Hyde Park Barracks
Art Gallery Of NSW

Martin Place

allan Nat.
laritime Mus.
Sydney Aquarium

York St.
Clarence St.
Pitt St.
Centrepoint Sydney Tower
Queen Victoria Building

Cowper Wharf Roadway
Challis St.
WOOLLOOMOOLOO

Pyrmont Bridge

Harbourside Festival Marketplace

Druitt St.
Bathurst St.
Liverpool St.
Goulburn St.

Clarence St.
York St.
Pitt St.
Castlereagh St.
Elizabeth St.
College St.
Park St.
Hyde Park
Australian Museum
Stanley
William St.
Haig Ave.
Sir John Young Cr.
Palmer
Bourke St.
Cathedral St.
Crown St.
Palmer
DARLINGHURST
KINGS CROSS
Darlinghurst Rd.
Victoria St.
Elizabeth Bay
Bayswater Rd.
William St.
Craigend St.

DARLING HARBOUR
Archibald Memorial Fountain
Anzac War Memorial

Chinese Garden

CHINATOWN

Darling Drive
Dixon St.
Sussex St.
George St.
Campbell St.
Wentworth Ave.
Oxford St.
Liverpool St.
Burton St.
Barcom Ave.
Greenknowe

The Power House Museum

Harris St.
Ultimo St.
Quay St.
George St.
Hay St.
Eddy Ave.
Campbell St.
Sydney Police Centre
Crown St.
Flinders St.
South Dowling St.
Oxford St.
Boundary St.

Belmore Park

Central Station

SURRY HILLS

N

0   400 m
0   400 y

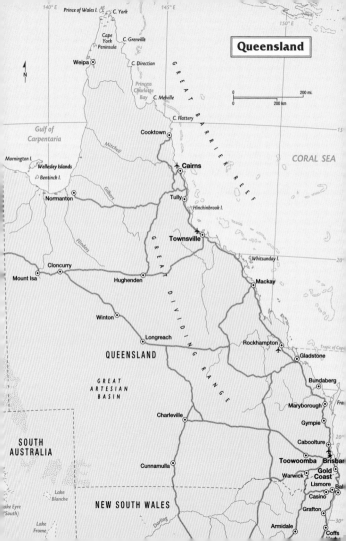

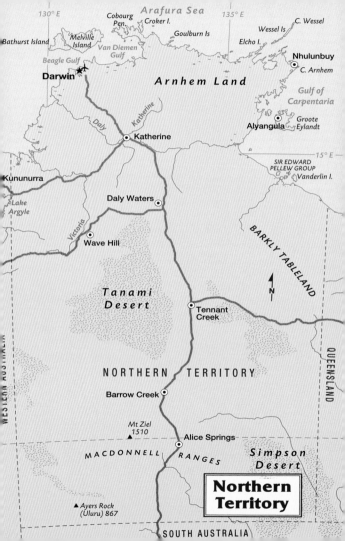

INDEX

founded in 1861, is the oldest such institution in the country. In comfortable modern surroundings it hits its stride with the wealth of Australian paintings from the 18th century to living masters. And remember to tilt your head back to admire the immense, 10,000-piece stained-glass ceiling of the Great Hall.

The Theatres Building, directly beneath the symbolic spire identifying the Arts Centre, is the place to see opera, ballet, and modern musicals. Under the same roof are a playhouse for drama and a smaller studio theater for performances of experimental works. The adjoining **Concert Hall,** which seats 2,700 people, is used for symphony concerts, but the acoustics can be changed to suit other types of performance. If you're not going to a concert, nip in for a glance at the artwork in the lobby, or take a guided backstage tour. The complex provides dining opportunities from snack bars to luxury-class restaurants.

Just across **Princes Bridge** on the north side of the river, the spires of **St. Paul's Cathedral** are not as old as they look. They were added in the 1920s, several decades after the original Gothic-style structure was completed. The church is a refreshing hideaway in the midst of the busiest part of the business district, a few steps away from the Victorian mass of the main railway station and a less obvious historic landmark, **Young & Jackson's** pub. In the bar upstairs hangs a notorious oil painting of the nude "Chloe" — which has delighted many generations of beer drinkers since it scandalized Melbourne's art exhibition of 1880. By today's standards, it's quite staid.

Just north of St. Paul's Cathedral, the city's new **Federation Square** is replacing former City Square. The new square, open at the end of 2001, houses a gallery dedicated to Australian art, along with various recreational amenities. It has been designed to become Melbourne's primary recreational and cultural space.

The Town Hall, on the opposite side of Collins Street, was built in the 1860s. Used for concerts and official happenings, it can hold 3,000 people.

Collins Street and the parallel Bourke Street are the reason Melburnians claim to have the best shopping in Australia. Three great department stores — Myer, David Jones, and Daimaru — are located conveniently close together, surrounded by small trendy shops, and a warren of arcades for making the most of those rainy hours. The outstanding example of an old-time Melbourne shopping institution, the glass-roofed **Block Arcade** is an 1892 copy of a Milan landmark, the Vittorio Emmanuele Galleria. **The Bourke Street Mall** is a pleasure to roam. Diversions are provided by clowns, magicians, bagpipers, and other hopefuls. But don't get carried away by the relaxed atmosphere: Although this is a pedestrians-only zone, there is one big exception — the trams rattle right down the middle of the mall.

By way of historic buildings, Melbourne likes to show off Parliament House, set in its own park facing Spring Street. It has been called the finest legislative headquarters this side of London; in fact, many of the furnishings found here are copies of those in Britain's Palace of Westminster. The federal government used this as its temporary headquarters in Australia's early days. The building, which dates from 1854, is open for guided tours when the state parliament is off duty.

Older than any of the city's well-preserved Victorian buildings is **Captain Cook's Cottage** in **Fitzroy Gardens.** The great discoverer never lived in Melbourne; the stone house was transplanted in 1934 from Great Ayton in Cook's native Yorkshire. In truth, it would be more accurate to call it Cook's *parents'* cottage, since there is no evidence that the good captain did live under its tile roof in his 18th-century childhood. The only genuine Cook relic in the place is a small sea chest with the initials J.C.

Only in Australia, it seems, are jails such popular tourist attractions. The most fascinating of all is the **Old Melbourne Gaol,** situated just across the street from the modern Police Headquarters on Russell Street. Opened in 1854, the three-story penitentiary was